SUZUKI A5 MOPEDS Owners Workshop Manual

by Jim Hammond

Models covered

A50P	First introduced into UK	September 1975
A50	First introduced into UK	February 1974
AS50	First introduced into UK	June 1969

ISBN 0 85696 328 3

© Haynes Publishing Group 1977

1657/328

Printed in England

Haynes Publishing Group
Sparkford Yeovil Somerset England
distributed in the USA by
Haynes Publications Inc
9421 Winnetka Avenue
Chatsworth
California 91311 USA

Acknowledgements

Our grateful thanks are due to Heron Suzuki (GB) Ltd for their technical advice and permission to use their drawings.

We are also grateful to the Avon Rubber Company, who so kindly provided illustrations and advice about tyre fitting and to the Champion Sparking Plug Co. Ltd. for the use of their illustrations about spark plug maintenance and electrode conditions.

Brian Horsfall assisted with the stripdown and rebuild of the machine featured and devised methods to overcome the need for service tools. The photographic work that accompanies the text was arranged and taken by Les Brazier. Gratitude must also be extended to Jeff Clew who edited the text.

We are especially grateful to Nick Barnes of the Heron Suzuki Technical Service Department for checking the content of this manual and suggesting ways in which the text could be improved. The machine featured throughout this manual was supplied by Fran Ridewood and Co. of Wells, whose assistance was very much appreciated.

About this manual

The author of this manual has the conviction that the only way in which a meaningful and easy to follow text can be written is first to do the work himself, under conditions similar to those found in the average household. As a result, the hands seen in the photographs are those of the author. Even the machine photographed was not new; an example that had covered several thousand miles was selected so that the conditions encountered would be similar to those found by the average rider. Unless specially mentioned, and therefore considered essential, Suzuki service tools have not been used. There is invariably some alternative means of slackening or removing some vital component when service tools are not available and risk of damage has to be avoided at all costs.

Each of the six Chapters is divided into numbered Sections. Within the Sections are numbered paragraphs. In consequence, cross reference throughout this manual is both straightforward and logical. When a reference is made 'See Section 15.12'.it means Section 5, paragraph 12 in the same Chapter. If another Chapter were meant, the text would read 'See Chapter 2, Sections 5.12'. All photographs are captioned with a Section/paragraph number to which they refer and are always relevant to the Chapter text adjacent.

Figure numbers (usually line illustrations) appear in numerical order, within a given Chapter. Fig. 1.1 therefore refers to the first figure in Chapter 1. Left-hand and right-hand descriptions of the machines and their component parts refer to the right and left of a given machine when the rider is seated normally.

Whilst every care is taken to ensure that the information in this manual is correct no liability can be accepted by the authors or publishers for loss, damage or injury caused by any errors in or omissions from the information given.

Contents

1977 SUZUKI A50P

1977 SUZUKI A50P

Introduction to the
Suzuki A50, A50P and AS50 models

At the time of publication there have been three versions of the 50 cc model. The engine/gearbox units of all three models have a very close similarity and utilise many of the same components. The main change has occurred with the A50P model, which is fitted with a set of pedals, and incorporates some minor changes such as the final drive gear ratios, carb-urettor jet sizes and the location and styling of the exhaust.

The machine actually stripped for the purpose of this manual was an A50P model and where differences occur between the various models, a note is made in the text, along with a note about any alteration in procedure that may be required.

Ordering spare parts

When ordering spare parts for any Suzuki, it is advisable to deal direct with an official Suzuki dealer who should be able to supply most of the parts ex-stock. Parts cannot be obtained from Suzuki direct and all orders must be routed via an approved dealer even if the parts required are not held in stock. Always quote the engine and frame numbers in full, especially if parts are required for earlier models.

The engine number is stamped on the upper rear of the crankcase, on the left-hand side.

The frame number is stamped along the right-hand side of the steering head. There is also a manufacturers' nameplate rivetted to the left-hand side of the steering head, on which the corresponding frame and engine numbers are stamped.

Always fit parts of genuine Suzuki manufacture and not pattern parts, which are often available at lower cost. Pattern parts do not necessarily make a satisfactory replacement for the originals and there are many cases where reduced life or sudden failure has occurred, to the detriment of performance.

Some of the more expendable parts such as spark plugs, bulbs, tyres, oils and greases etc., can be obtained from accessory shops and motor factors, who have convenient opening hours, charge lower prices and can often be found not far from home. It is also possible to obtain parts on Mail Order basis from a number of specialists who advertise regularly in the motor cycle magazines.

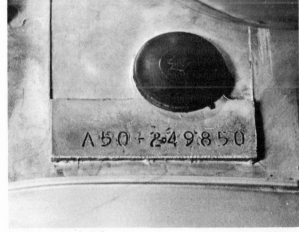

Engine number location

Frame Number location

Manufacturers nameplate location

Routine maintenance

Periodic routine maintenance is a continuous process that begins immediately the machine is used. It must be carried out at specified mileage recordings or on a calander basis if the machine is not used frequently, whichever is the soonest. Maintenance should always be regarded as an insurance policy to help keep the machine in the peak of condition and to ensure long, trouble-free service. It has the additional benefit of giving early warning of any faults that may develop and will act as a safety check, to the obvious benefit of both rider and machine alike.

The various maintenance tasks are described under their respective mileage and calandar headings. Accompanying diagrams are provided, where necessary. It should be remembered that the interval between the various maintenance tasks serves only as a guide. As the machine gets older or is used under particularly adverse conditions, it is advisable to reduce the period between each check.

No special tools are required for the normal routine maintenance tasks. The tools contained in the tool kit supplied with every new machine will prove adequate for each task, but if they are not available, the following list will suffice.

Set of metric open ended spanners from 6 mm to 12 mm
Plug spanner
Pair of pliers
Medium size screwdriver
Feeler gauges
Small electrical screwdriver
5 mm Allen key
Adjustable spanner
Box spanner, 10 mm and 11 mm with tommy bar
Crosshead screwdriver
Tyre pressure gauge
Tyre pump

When buying tools it is worth spending a little more than the minimum to ensure that good quality tools are obtained. Some of the cheaper tools are too soft or flimsy to do an adequate job. It is infuriating to have to stop part way through a job because a spanner has splayed open or broken, and a replacement must be found.

A deep-rooted knowledge of engineering principles is by no means necessary before the owner undertakes his own routine maintenance tasks, but familiarity with a few of the more commonly used terms and a basic knowledge of how to use tools will help.

Weekly or every 200 miles

1 Check the oil level through the inspection window in the oil tank. If the level is low, it must be topped up with a recommended two-stroke oil.

2 *Check the tyre pressures (tyres cold)*
A50 and A50P models

Tyre	Solo riding	Dual riding
Front	25 psi (1.75 kg/cm^2)	25 psi (1.75 kg/cm^2)
Rear	28 psi (2.0 kg/cm^2)	39 psi (2.8 kg/cm^2)

AS50 model

Tyre	Solo riding	Dual riding
Front	22 psi (1.5 kg/cm^2)	22 psi (1.5 kg/cm^2)
Rear	29 psi (2.0 kg/cm^2)	34 psi (2.4 kg/cm^2)

Remove the dust cap, depress the centre valve and release quickly, to blow out any dust or water, and push on the tyre pressure gauge. If the pressure is too low, increase it using a pump or garage air line, to the correct pressure. If pressure is too high, depress valve centre and release air until the correct pressure is reached, by rechecking with a tyre pressure gauge.

Replace the dust cap as it acts as a second seal as well as keeping out dust and moisture.

Check the oil level through the inpsection window

Top-up with recommended lubricant if level is low

Turn the front brake cable adjusting nut

Turn the adjusting nut

Note the amount of brake lining wear

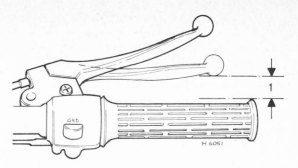

Front brake adjustment

1   0.8 - 1.2 in (20 - 30 mm)

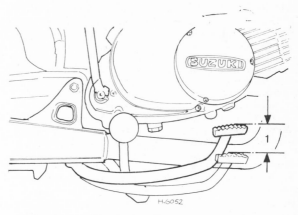

Rear brake adjustment

1   0.8 - 1.2 in (20 - 30 mm)

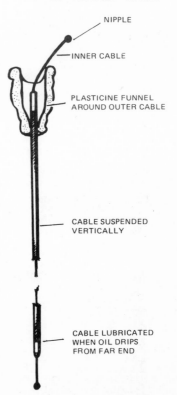

NIPPLE

INNER CABLE

PLASTICINE FUNNEL
AROUND OUTER CABLE

CABLE SUSPENDED
VERTICALLY

CABLE LUBRICATED
WHEN OIL DRIPS
FROM FAR END

CONTROL CABLE OILING

3 Oil the brake cable and adjust the brakes

Brakes are items of personal safety and must always be correctly adjusted.

Oil the cable at the cable ends and pivot points, using a light machine oil.

Front brake adjustment

Measure the distance between the brake lever and throttle twist grip when brake is applied. This dimension should be 20 to 30 mm (0.8 to 1.2 inches). If adjustment is necessary, turn the brake cable adjusting nut along the thread to achieve the correct dimension at the brake lever.

Rear brake

Check the free travel of the rear brake pedal. Normal free travel is 20 to 30 mm (0.8 to 1.2 inches). If adjustment is necessary, turn the adjusting nut clockwise to decrease the free travel and anticlockwise to increase it.

Note the amount of brake lining wear that has taken place by checking the movement of the brake operating arm relative to the range scale marked on both brake plates. The brake lining need not be renewed as long as the engraved line on the brake operating arm is within the range scale.

4 Oil and adjust the clutch cable

Oil the cable ends and lever pivots, using a light machine oil. Adjust play at the handlebar lever, which should be 4 mm (0.16 inches), before the clutch begins to disengage. If play is incorrect, adjust as follows:

 a) Slide the rubber dust cover a short way up the cable.
 b) Loosen the clutch adjusting screw locknut.
 c) Turn the cable adjuster until a gap of 4 mm (0.16 inches) is obtained at the clutch lever.
 d) Tighten the cable adjuster locknut and replace the dust cover.

5 Battery check

Remove the battery compartment cover, located on the left-hand-side, and check the level of the electrolyte. If the level is low, remove the two screws to release the battery holder, slide the battery part-way out and remove the vent plugs from the top of the battery. Using distilled water, not water from the tap, top up the battery to the correct level, and replace the vent plugs. Do not overfill. If any of the battery electrolyte is spilt, it must be washed off immediately with fresh water as it will quickly corrode metal and burn the skin. Replace the battery and refit the battery holder and compartment cover.

6 Check the lights and horn

Check that all lights, including the indicators, are working properly. Replace any defective bulbs with new items and if any lights are dim, clean their connections and earthing points, to restore the lights to their correct brightness.

Check the horn for correct operation. If performance is poor check the connections.

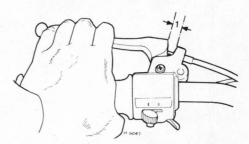

Clutch lever adjustment

1   0.16 in (4 mm)

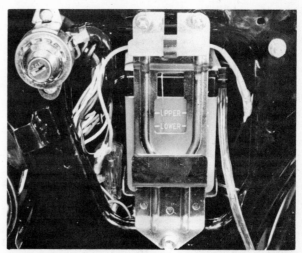

Check the level of the electrolyte

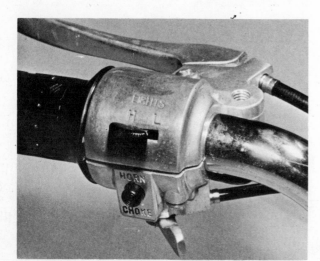

Check the lights and horn and ...

... the indicators

Remove the cup and O ring

Check tightness of the ring nut

Monthly or every 1,000 miles (1,600 km)

Complete all the checks listed in the weekly/200 mile service and then the following items:

1 Check the spark plug

An NGK B-8HS or Nippon Denso W24FS spark plug is fitted as standard equipment and the recommended gap is 0.6 to 0.7 mm (0.024 to 0.028 inches)

Pull off the spark plug cap and using the correct size plug spanner, remove the plug. Clean off any carbon or oil from the electrodes and using feeler gauges, check the gap. Reset the gap, if necessary, after referring to Chapter 3. Refit the spark plug into the cylinder head but do not overtighten it, as stripping of the threads could result. Refit the plug cap.

A new spark plug should be fitted every 5,000 miles (8,000 km) or earlier, if it is excessively worn, burnt or damaged.

2 Adjust slow running speed

Adjust the slow running speed only if necessary. Refer to Chapter 2, Section 5.

3 Check and adjust the contact breaker gap

The correct setting of the contact breaker gap is critical and engine performance can be adversly affected if it is not carried out correctly. Refer to Chapter 3, Section 5 for the relevant details.

4 Clean the fuel tap filter

Ensure the fuel tap filter is clean so that a smooth flow of fuel passes through the fuel tap. Turn the fuel tap to the OFF position. Using a 10 mm spanner, remove the cup and 'O' ring. Remove the filter gauge and wash it in clean petrol. Refit the filter 'O' ring and cup. Tighten the cup, using a 10 mm spanner. Remember to turn the fuel top ON before attempting to start the engine.

5 Exhaust pipe ring nut

Check the tightness of the ring nut at the cylinder barrel.

6 Lubricate the final drive chain

Lubricate the final drive chain, using SAE 90 oil. Application of the oil is made easier by the use of an aerosol pack of chain lubricant.

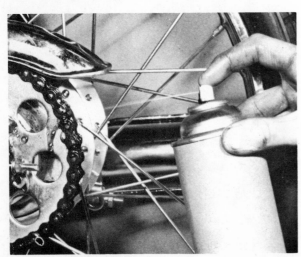
Lubricate the final drive chain

Remove the pedal chain cover

Three monthly or every 2,000 miles (3,000 km)

Complete all the checks listed in the weekly/200 mile and monthly/1,000 mile services, and then the following additional tasks.

1 Oil pump - check and adjust

Oil is fed by the oil pump to the crankshaft big-end and small-end bearings, the piston and cylinder walls. The amount of oil fed to these areas is regulated by the oil pump control lever, which is operated by the amount of throttle opening and engine speed. Remove the pedal original drive chain cover, left-hand crankcase cover and the oil pump cover (Chapter 1, Fully open the throttle and check that the marks on the control lever align with the mark on pump body, the top section of the dot mark on the carburettor slide should be aligned with the top of the carburettor bore. If alignment is incorrect, loosen the cable locknut and turn adjuster until the marks are aligned. Retighten the locknut and refit the covers.

2 Cylinder head nuts - check and tighten

Check and if necessary tighten the cylinder head nuts (10mm). The torque setting should be 7.2 ft lb (100 kg cm).

3 Clean the air filter

If the air cleaner filter becomes blocked, intake resistance increases, resulting in loss of power and an increase in fuel consumption.

Remove the dome nut, nylon washer and cover from the air cleaner assembly and take out the air filter element. Using air pressure or a brush, clean off any dirt and dust. If the element is clogged or damaged, renew it. Replace the filter, fit the cover, nylon washer and dome nut.

4 Final drive chain - check and adjust the tension

Place the machine on its centre stand. Check the up and down movement of the chain, midway between the two sprockets. Slowly rotate the rear wheel until the up and down movement is at a minimum. This is the tight-spot and the up and down movement must be between 15 to 20 mm (0.6 and 0.8 inches). If necessary, adjust the chain by removing the split pin, loosening the rear wheel nut and the sprocket drum nut. Turn each chain adjuster nut to the same index mark each side of the swinging arm fork for correct wheel alignment and for the correct up and down chain tension. Tighten the sprocket drum nut and rear wheel nut. Recheck the play in the chain, then replace the split pin through the rear wheel nut. Note that the rod-operated rear brake should be checked and if necessary, adjusted after any

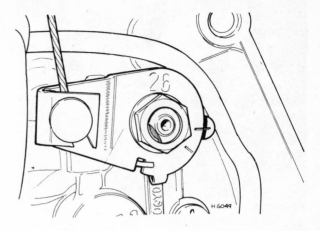

(A) Drawing of alignment of oil pump marks

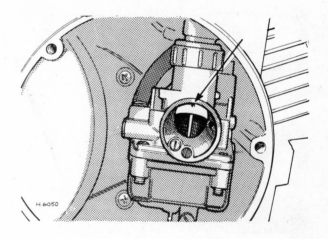

(B) Drawing of punch mark on carburettor slide

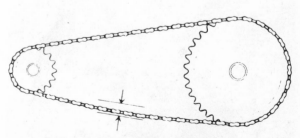

0.6 - 0.8 in (15 - 20 mm)

Checking final drive chain

Take out the filter element

Remove the split pin

Turn each chain adjuster nut

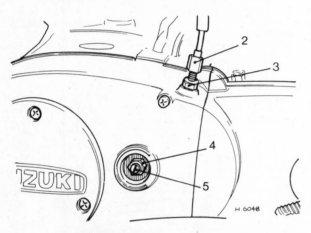
Clutch pushrod adjustment

2 Clutch cable adjuster   4 Locknut
3 Lock nut   5 Screw

Remove spring link when on the rear wheel sprocket

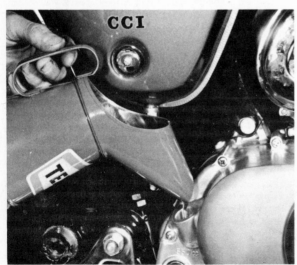
Refill the gearbox

Drain excess oil before replacing the level plug screw

chain adjustments. See weekly/200 mile service, item 3.

5 Adjust the clutch

Remove the pedal and final drive chain cover to expose the clutch adjusting rod and locknut.

Loosen the locknut and using a screwdriver, turn the adjusting rod in (clockwise) until it just touches the push-rod; turn it out (anticlockwise) half-a-turn. Maintaining the adjusting rod in this position, tighten the locknut. Adjust the clutch cable as described in the weekly/200 mile service.

6 Check the contact breaker points gap

To check, and if necessary adjust the contact breaker points gap, remove the two inspection cover screws and the cover, found on the left-hand side of the machine. Rotate the flywheel until the contact breaker points, viewed through one of the apertures cut in the face of the flywheel rotor, are in the fully open position. The correct gap should be within the range 0.3 - 0.4 mm (0.012 - 0.016 inch). If the locknut and turning it either clockwise or anti-clockwise, depending on whether the gap needs to be increased or decreased. When the setting is correct, the feeler gauge should be a good sliding fit. Tighten the locknut and re-check the gap.

If the points are burnt or in generally poor condition, further attention is required, as detailed in Section of Chapter 3.

7 Check the ignition timing

If the ignition timing is correct, the contact breaker points should be about to separate as the mark on the flywheel rotor rim aligns exactly with the cast pointer of the engine crankcase, found in approximately the 8 o'clock position. These marks constitute only a rough guide. If there is reason to suspect the ignition timing is not correct, refer to Section 6 of Chapter 3 for further information.

Note that the contact breaker gap must always be set correctly first, before the accuracy of the ignition timing is verified. It should also be noted that even a small discrepency in the ignition timing will have a marked effect on engine performance.

Six monthly or every 4,000 miles (6,000 km)

Complete all the checks listed in the weekly/200, monthly/1,000 mile and three montly/2000 mile services and then the following additional tasks:

1 Oil the contact breaker cam felt pad

When checking the contact breaker points gap, the felt pad can be seen through one of the flywheel apertures. Lubricate the felt pad with a few drops of light machine oil to reduce wear on the heel of the points. Do not over oil, or excess oil will find its way on to the points and cause ignition problems.

2 Lubricate the final drive and pedal chains

To remove the chains, place the machine on the centre stand. On the A50P model, remove the three screws securing the pedal chain cover, from the left-hand side of the machine and remove the cover. Allow it to rest on the left-hand pedal.

Remove the U shaped spring clip from the link plate, remove the side plate and push out the link plate, parting the chain. Remove the chain from both sprockets.

On the A50 and AS50 models, remove the screws securing the final drive sprocket cover and remove the cover. Remove the screws securing the chain casing, which is in two parts, and remove the casing.

On all models, revolve the rear wheel until the spring link is on the rear sprocket. Disconnect the chain as in the case of the pedal chain and remove it from the machine. Wash the chains thoroughly in petrol or paraffin to remove all dirt and grease.

To check whether a chain is due for renewal, lay it length-ways in a straight line and compress it at each end to take up all play. Anchor one end and pull on the other end to extend the chain and take up all play in the other direction. If the chain extends by more than the distance between two of the rollers it should be renewed and a close examination of both the engine and rear wheel sprockets must be carried out, to check for wear and sprocket tooth damage. The dismantling procedure for renewal of the sprockets, if found to be necessary, is given in Chapter 1, Sections 11 and 45.

The chain must be lubricated after cleaning, by immersing it in a molten chain lubricant, such as Linklyfe or Chainguard and then hanging it up to drain. This will ensure good penetration of the lubricant between the pins and rollers, making it less likely to be thrown off when the chain is in motion.

To refit the final drive chain, feed it first onto the gearbox sprocket. On A50P models this may prove slightly more difficult as the gearbox sprocket is behind the left-hand engine casing. If this operation proves too difficult, refer to Chapter 1, Sections 1 to 14 and 1 to 46 for removal and installation of the left-hand engine casing.

Position the two ends of the chain on the rear wheel sprocket, insert the link, fit the side plate and secure with the spring clip. Note that the closed end of the spring clip must be fitted pointing in the direction of motion.

Adjust the chain tension as previously stated in the three monthly service.

3 Change the transmission oil

It is better to change the transmission oil when it is hot, and the viscosity is lower.

Place the machine on its centre stand and position a suitable container under the gearbox oil drain plug. Remove the plug and the oil filler cap and allow the oil to drain. Check the condition of the drain plug sealing washer and when the flow of oil has ceased, wipe the area around the hole, refit and tighten the plug. Remove the oil level screw and refill the garbox with oil of the correct viscosity, until oil starts to flow from the level plug hole. Allow the excess to drain off, then fit the level plug and the oil filler cap. It is essential the machine is standing on level ground throughout this operation.

4 Check the condition of the brake linings

Although a brake lining wear indicator is provided on some models, it is advisable to remove both wheels from the machine, in turn, in order to check the condition of the brake drum and the extent to which the brake linings have worn. Since this will entail a small amount of dismantling, reference should be made to Chapter 5 for information about the removal of the front wheel (Section 3) or the rear wheel (Section 5). Visual inspection will show whether the brake linings require attention, and it is recommended that reference is made to Section 6 of the same Chapter if it is necessary to remove the brake shoe assembly from either wheel.

Twelve monthly or every 8,000 miles (12,000 km)

Complete all the checks listed under the weekly, monthly, three and six monthly headings, but only if they are not directly connected with the tasks listed below. More extensive dismantling is required when undertaking these latter tasks and reference to the relevant Chapters and Sections will be necessary in each case:

1 Dismantle, clean, examine and reassemble the carburettor.
2 Renew the contact breaker assembly.
3 Remove both wheels, grease the bearings and brake operating cams.
4 Check and grease the steering head bearings.
5 Decarbonise the engine and clean the exhaust system, especially the silencer.

Dimensions, weight and capacities

Model	A50 Imperial	A50 Metric	AS50 Imperial	AS50 Metric	A50P Imperial	A50P Metric
Wheelbase	46.7 in	1185 mm	45.1 in	1160 mm	47.2 in	1200 mm
Overall length	70.9 in	1800 mm	70.3 in	1785 mm	71.7 in	1820 mm
Overall width	29.9 in	760 mm	24.8 in	630 mm	30.1 in	765 mm
Overall height	38.6 in	980 mm	35.3 in	895 mm	40.2 in	1020 mm
Ground clearance (unladen)	4.9 in	125 mm	5.9 in	150 mm		
Weight, dry (unladen) ...	165 lb	75 kg	160 lb	63 kg		
Fuel tank, total	1.6 gall	7.5 litres	1.43 gall	6.5 litres	1.6 gall	7.5 litres
Fuel tank, reserve ...	3.6 pt	2 litres	1.8 pt	1 litre	3.6 pt	2 litres
Oil tank capacity (engine)	2.1 pt	1.2 litres	2.72 pt	1.6 litres	2.1 pt	1.2 litres
Gearbox capacity	1 pt	550 cc	1 pt	550 cc	1 pt	550 cc
Front fork leg (each) ...	0.23 Imp pints	133 cc	0.23 Imp pints	133 cc	0.23 Imp pints	133 cc

Recommended lubricants and fluids

Component	Grade	Description
Engine oil (oil tank)	SAE 30	Non diluent two-stroke oil
Gearbox/transmission oil	SAE 20W/50	
Front forks	SAE 10W/30	Automatic Transmission Fluid
Final drive chain	... ...	Heavyweight motor oil or proprietary chain lubricant
Control cables	... ...	Light oil
All greasing points	... ...	Proprietary lithium base grease

For specific lubricant recommendations apply to Heron Suzuki GB Limited Technical Department

Working conditions and tools

When a major overhaul is contemplated, it is important that a clean, well-lit working space is available, equipped with a workbench and vice, and with space for laying out or storing the dismantled assemblies in an orderly manner where they are unlikely to be disturbed. The use of a good workshop will give the satisfaction of work done in comfort and without haste, where there is little chance of the machine being dismantled and reassembled in anything other than clean surroundings. Unfortunately, these ideal working conditions are not always practicable and under these latter circumstances when improvisation is called for, extra care and time will be needed.

The other essential requirement is a comprehensive set of good quality tools. Quality is of prime importance, since cheap tools will prove expensive in the long run if they slip or break and damage the components to which they are applied. A good quality tool will last a long time, and more than justify the cost. The basis of any tool kit is a set of open-ended spanners, which can be used on almost any part of the machine to which there is reasonable access. A set of ring spanners makes a useful addition. since they can be used on nuts that are very tight of where access is restricted. Where the cost has to be kept within reasonable bounds, a compromise can be effected with a set of combination spanners - open-ended at one end and having a ring of the same size on the other end. Socket spanners may also be considered a good investment, a basic ½ inch drive kit comprising a ratchet handle and a small number of socket heads, if money is limited. Additional sockets can be purchased, as and

when they are required. Provided they are slim in profile, sockets will reach nuts or bolts that are deeply recessed. When purchasing spanners of any kind, make sure that the correct size standard is purchased. Almost all machines manufactured outside the UK and the USA have metric nuts and bolts, whilst those produced in Britain have BSF or BSW sizes. The standard used in the USA is AF, which is also found on some of the later British machines. Other tools that should be included in the kit are a range of crosshead screwdrivers, a pair of pliers and a hammer.

When considering the purchase of tools, it should be remembered that by carrying out the work oneself, a large proportion of the normal repair cost, made up by labour charges, will be saved. The economy made on even a minor overhaul will go a long way towards the improvement of a tool kit.

In addition to the basic tool kit, certain additional tools can prove invaluable when they are close to hand, to help speed up a multitude of repetitive jobs. For example, an impact screwdriver will ease the removal of screws that have been tightened by a similar tool, during assembly, without risk of damaging the screw heads. And, of course, it can be used again to retighten the screws, to ensure an oil or airtight seal results. Circlip pliers have their uses too, since gear pinions, shafts and similar components are frequently retained by circlips that are not too easily displaced by a screwdriver. There are two types of circlip plier, one for internal and one for external circlips. They may also have straight or right-angled jaws.

One of the most useful of all tools is the torque wrench, a form of spanner that can be adjusted to slip when a measured amount of force is applied to any bolt or nut. Torque wrench settings are given in almost every modern workshop or service manual, where the extent to which a complex component, such as a cylinder head, can be tightened without fear of distortion or leakage. The tightening of bearing caps is yet another example. Overtightening will stretch or even break bolts, necessitating extra work to extract the broken portions.

As may be expected, the more sophisicated the machine, the greater is the number of tools likely to be required if it is to be kept in first class condition by the home mechanic. Unfortunately, there are certain jobs which cannot be accomplished successfully without the correct equipment and although there is invariably a specialist who will undertake the work for a fee, the home mechanic will have to dig more deeply in his pocket for the purchase of similar equipment if he does not wish to employ the services of others. Here a word of caution is necessary, since some of these jobs are best left to the expert. Although an electrical multimeter of the Avo type will prove helpful in tracing electrical faults, in inexperienced hands it may irrevocably damage some of the electrical components if a test current is passed through them in the wrong direction. This can apply to the synchronisation of twin or multiple carburettors too, where a certain amount of expertise is needed when setting them up with vacuum gauges. These are, however, exceptions. Some instruments, such as a strobe lamp, are virtually essential when checking the timing of a machine powered by a CD ignition system. In short, do not purchase any of these special items unless you have the experience to use them correctly.

Although this manual shows how components can be removed and replaced without the use of special service tools (unless absolutely essential), it is worthwhile giving consideration to the purchase of the more commonly used tools if the machine is regarded as a long term purchase. Whilst the alternative methods suggested will remove and replace parts without risk of damage, the use of the special tools recommended and sold by the manufacturer will invariably save time.

Torque wrench settings

	Tightening torque	
	kg cm	lb ft
Spark plug	200 - 240	14 - 17
Cylinder head nuts	100	7.2
Oil pump union bolts	20 - 30	1.4 - 2.0
Steering stem head fitting bolt	180 - 280	13 - 20
Fork fitting bolts	180 - 280	13 - 20
Handlebar clamp bolts	60 - 90	4.0 - 6.5
Front wheel spindle nut	360 - 440	26 - 32
Rear wheel spindle nut	270 - 330	20 - 24
Rear shock absorber upper bolts	180 - 280	13 - 20
Rear shock absorber lower bolts	180 - 280	13 - 20
Swinging arm pivot shaft	180 - 280	13 - 20
Front fork stanchion fitting bolts	180 - 280	13 - 20
Rear wheel sprocket mounting nuts	450 - 500	33 - 43
Engine mounting bolts	130 - 230	9.5 - 17
Check valve	30 - 50	2.0 - 3.6
Oil level inspection lens screw	16 - 20	1.2 - 1.5
Oil pump securing screw	30 - 50	2.0 - 3.6
Flywheel generator retaining nut	350 - 450	25 - 33

Chapter 1 Engine, Clutch and Gearbox

Contents

Specifications

Engine

Type	Single cylinder, two stroke, air cooled
Capacity	49 cc (2.99 cu in)
Bore	41 mm (1.62 in)
Stroke	37.8 mm (1.49 in)
Corrected compression ratio	6.7 : 1
Maximum horsepower	4.9 @ 8500 rpm
Maximum torque	0.43 kg m (3.11 lb f ft) @ 8000 rpm
Starter	Kick only

Clutch

Type	Wet, multi-plate
No. of friction plates	4
No. of plain plates	4
Primary drive	
type	Helical gear
reduction ratio	3.84 : 1 (73/19)
Final drive ratio	2.66 : 1 (32/12) A50M (37/14)

Gearbox

									5-speed constant mesh	
Type	...	...	...	...	...	...	...	...		
Ratios									A50P	A50
1st	...	...	...	...	...	...	...	...	3.75 : 1 (45/12)	3.667 (44/12)
2nd	...	...	...	...	...	...	...	...	2.16 : 1 (39/18)	2.133 (32/15)
3rd	...	...	...	...	...	...	...	...	1.59 : 1 (35/22)	1.579 (30/19)
4th	...	...	...	...	...	...	...	...	1.28 : 1 (32/25)	1.280 (32/25)
5th	...	...	...	...	...	...	...	...	1.07 : 1 (30/28)	1.071 (30/28)

Dimensions and wear limits

	Metric (mm)	Imperial (in)
Standard cylinder bore	40.860 - 40.875	1.6118 - 1.6094
(measured 5 mm (0.197 in) above exhaust port)		
Wear limit	0.05	0.002
Piston/bore clearance	0.065 - 0.075	0.0026 - 0.0027
(measured 23 mm (0.906 in) up from the bottom of piston skirt)		
Wear limit	0.125	0.0049
Piston ring end gap	0.1 - 0.3	0.0039 - 0.0118
Wear limit	1.5	0.059
Clutch plate thickness (friction)	2.9 - 3.1	0.114 - 0.122
Wear limit	2.8	0.110
Clutch plate warpage (friction)	under 0.4	0.016
Wear limit	0.4	0.016
Clutch plate warpage (plain)	under 0.1	0.004
Wear limit	0.1	0.004
Clutch spring free length	32.9	1.295
Wear limit	34.1	1.343
Primary drive backlash	0.01 - 0.08	0.0004 - 0.0032
Wear limit	0.15	0.0059
Crank shaft axial alignment	under 0.05	0.0020
Wear limit	0.1	0.0039
Clutch housing axial play	0.01 - 0.25	0.0004 - 0.0098
Wear limit	0.3	0.0118
Gear change pawl return spring free length	24.3	0.957
Wear limit	27	1.063
Gear change cam stopper spring free length	17	0.669
Wear limit	20	0.787
Drive shaft bush inside diameter	12 - 12.02	0.4724 - 0.4732
Wear limit	12.06	0.4748

1 General description

The Suzuki A50, AS50 and A50P models are all fitted with an air cooled, single cylinder two-stroke engine. Engine lubrication is by the Suzuki CCI system. Transmission is by helical gear to a wet multiplate clutch which drives a 5-speed gearbox.

2 Operations with the engine/gearbox in the frame

It is not necessary to remove the engine/gearbox unit from the frame unless the crankshaft assembly and/or gearbox compartment need attention. Most operations can be accomplished with the engine/gearbox in place, such as:
  a) Removal and installation of the cylinder head
  b) Removal and installation of the cylinder barrel and piston.
  c) Removal and installation of the flywheel generator and contact breaker assembly.
  d) Removal and installation of the clutch.
  e) Removal and installation of the kickstart spring.
When several operations need to be undertaken at the same time, it would probably be advantageous to remove the complete unit from the frame, a comparitively simple operation. This will afford better access and more working space.

3 Engine/gearbox: removal from frame

1 Remove three screws from the cover over the carburettor, on the right-hand side and remove the cover.
2 Remove the four screws from the carburettor top cover and ease the cover up the cables.

3 Using a screwdriver, loosen the clamp bolt securing the carburettor to its stub and remove the carburettor.
4 Unscrew the carburettor top and starter cable adjuster (choke). Pull off the fuel line after first turning off the fuel at the tap.
5 Loosen the air cleaner clamp fitting bolt and remove the air cleaner assembly.

3.2 Remove the four screws from the cover

3.3 Loosen the clamp bolt

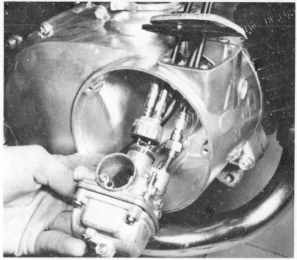

3.4 Unscrew the carburettor top

3.5 Loosen the air cleaner clamp fitting bolt

3.7a Remove the nut securing the exhaust system to the frame

3.7b Unscrew the nut securing the exhaust to the cylinder barrel

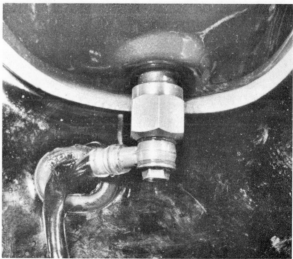

3.9 Disconnect the oil feed banjo

6   Remove the spark plug cap from the spark plug.

7   Remove the nut and washer securing the exhaust system to the frame, on the right-hand side of the machine. Unscrew the nut securing the exhaust to the cylinder barrel, remove the complete exhaust assembly and exhaust pipe gasket.

8   Remove the nut and bolt securing the kickstart lever to its shaft and the kickstart lever itself.

9   Disconnect the oil pipe banjo connection at the oil tank and either drain the oil into clean container or temporarily plug the hole, using a 6 mm screw.

10 Remove the pedal chain case which is secured by three screws (A50P model).

11 Remove the pedal chain and front sprocket by removing the circlip, sprocket, spring and splined wheel from the drive shaft. Disconnect the pedal chain at its spring link (A50P model).

12 Scribe a mark on the gearchange lever and shaft for ease of assembly, loosen the securing bolt and remove the gearchange lever.

13 Disconnect the final drive chain by removing the spring link.

14 Remove the six screws and the left-hand engine cover.

15 Push up on the clutch release screw lever in the engine cover and disconnect the cable inner and split nipple.

3.11a Remove the circlip

3.11b Draw off the pedal sprocket and spring ...

3.11c ... and splined dog

3.15a Take off the left-hand engine cover

3.15b Disconnect the cable inner and split nipple

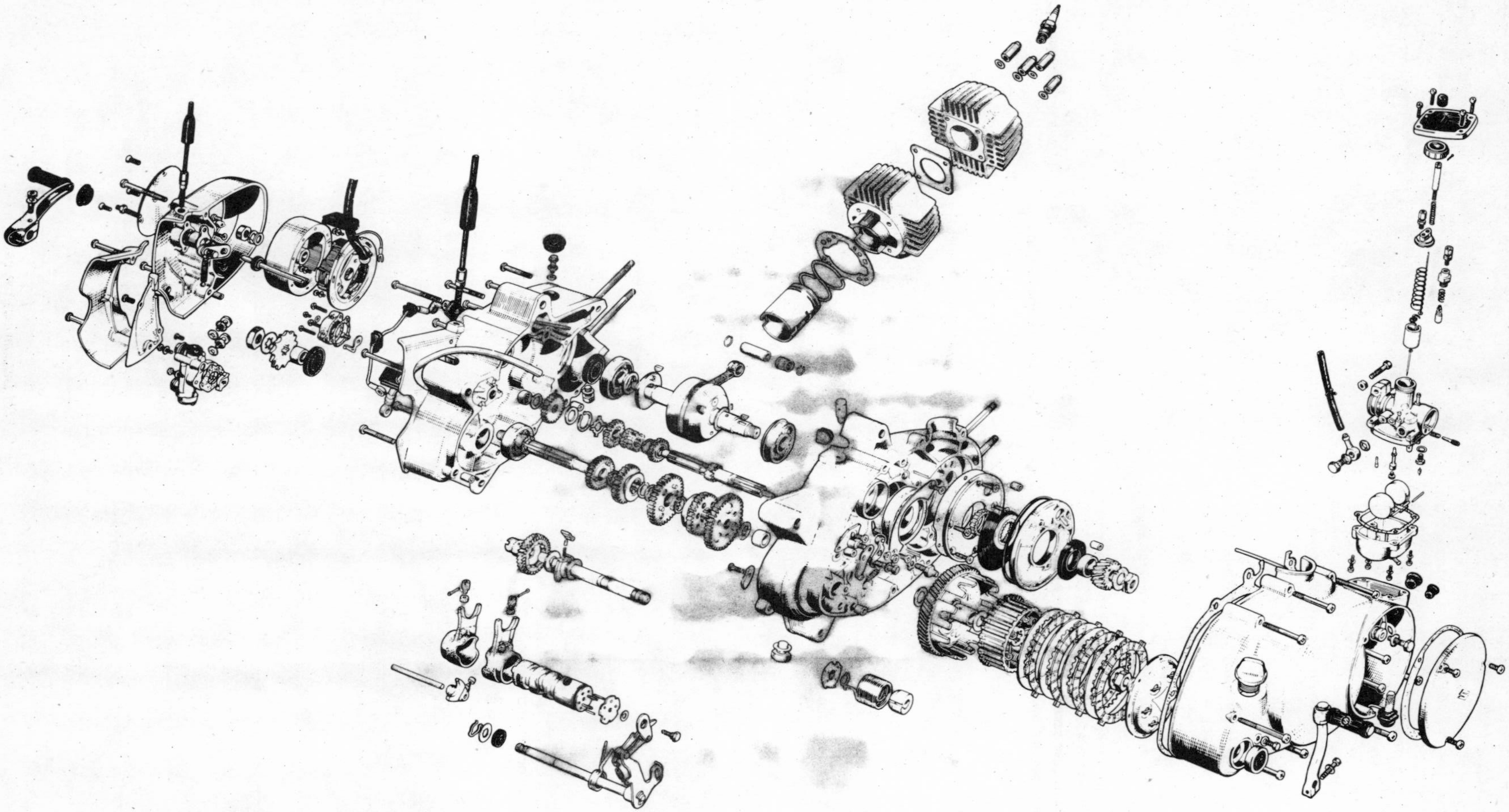

Fig. 1.1. SUZUKI A50 and SUZUKI SPORT AS50 engine

16 Loosen the adjuster locknut and remove the clutch cable
and adjuster from the left-hand engine cover.
17 Remove one screw from the oil pump and cover, then remove
the cover.
18 Disconnect the throttle/oil pump cable from the oil pump
at the split nipple. Loosen the adjuster locknut and remove the
cable.
19 Remove the battery cover from the left-hand side of the
machine, remove the three screws securing the battery and
cover and ease the battery out of its compartment. Remove the
plastic vent pipe and disconnect the two battery leads.
20 From inside the battery compartment, locate the main
wiring loom. Disconnect the black, green, yellow and blue
leads at their snap connectors.
21 Apart from the three engine support nuts and bolts,
the engine/gearbox unit is ready to be removed from the
frame. Remove the three nuts, and supporting the engine/
gearbox unit, withdraw the 3 bolts. Carefully guide the wiring
loom, previously disconnected, from the frame, and at the same
time, guide the engine oil pipe line clear from the right-hand
side of the machine.

4 Dismantling the engine, clutch and gearbox: general

Before commencing work on the engine unit, the external
surfaces should be cleaned thoroughly. A motor cycle engine has
very little protection from road grit and other foreign matter,
which will find its way into the dismantled engine if this simple
precaution is not observed. One of the proprietary cleaning
compounds such as 'Gunk' can be used to good effect,
particularly if the compound is allowed to work into the film of
oil and grease before it is washed away. When washing down,
make sure that water cannot enter the carburettor or the
electrical system, particularly if these parts have been exposed.

Never use undue force to remove any stubborn parts, unless
mention is made of this requirement. There is invariably good
reason why a part is difficult to remove, often because the
dismantling operation has been tackled in the wrong sequence.
Dismantling will be made easier if a simple engine stand is
constructed that will correspond with the engine mounting
points. This arrangement will permit the complete unit to be
clamped rigidly to the workbench, leaving both hands free.

3.17 Remove the oil pump cover

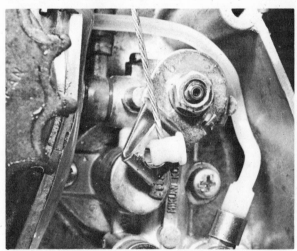
3.18 Disconnect the throttle/oil pump cable

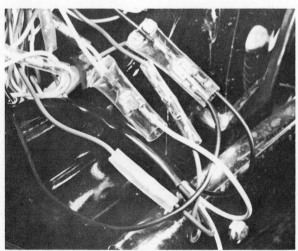
3.20 Disconnect at the electrical connectors

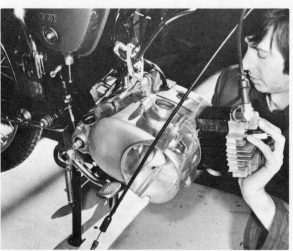
3.21 Support the engine/gearbox unit

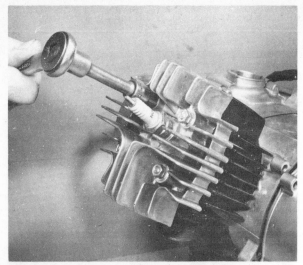

6.1a Slacken off the four cylinder head nuts and ...

6.1b ... lift off the cylinder head

6.1c Remove the head gasket

7.1 Lift off the cylinder barrel

8.1 Remove and discard both circlips

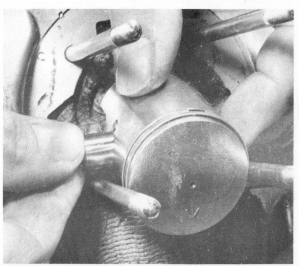

8.2 Push out the gudgeon pin

8.4 Note the arrow on the piston crown

8.5 Push out the needle roller small end

8.6 Support the connecting rod

9.2 Use a two-leg puller

5 Preventing the engine from turning both for dismantling and reassembly purposes

1   It is often necessary to stop the engine from rotating so that a component can be removed or tightened eg; engine sprocket nut or clutch centre nut. One way of achieving this that can be used during dismantling and reassembly is by placing a round metal bar through the small end boss and resting this bar on two pieces of wood placed on top of the crankcase mouth. On no account must the metal bar be allowed to bear directly down onto the gasket face of the crankcase mouth, otherwise damage will occur and cause a loss of primary compression.

6 Cylinder head: removal

1   To prevent distortion, slacken off the four cylinder head nuts in a diagonal sequence. Remove the nuts and washers and lift off the cylinder head. Remove the cylinder head gasket.
2   Remove the spark plug.

7 Cylinder barrel: removal

1   Lift off the cylinder barrel whilst supporting the connecting rod and piston. Stuff the crankcase mouth with rags to prevent anything being dropped into the engine and to protect the edges. If the cylinder barrel is stuck, tap gently around the joint with a soft faced hammer.

8 Piston and small end: removal

1   Remove both of the circlips retaining the gudgeon pin and discard them. They must never be reused.
2   Push out the gudgeon pin from the piston and release the piston from the connecting rod.
3   If the gudgeon pin is tight, warm the piston by wrapping it in a rag, soaked in boiling water and rung out. Never drift the gudgeon pin out unless absolutely necessary, and only then if the piston is well supported, otherwise there is risk of bending the connecting rod.
4   Note that the piston crown is marked with an arrow and when reassembling, this arrow must point forwards, towards the exhaust port.
5   Push out the small end needle roller bearing.
6   Remove the cylinder barrel gasket and discard it.

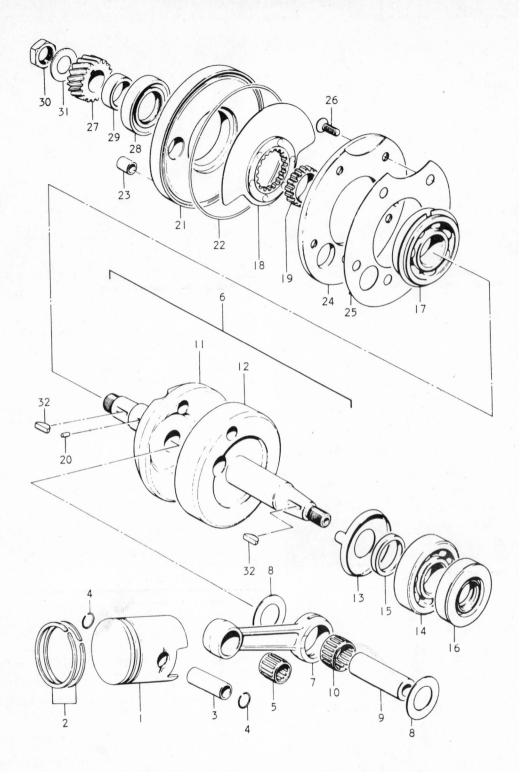

Fig. 1.2. Piston and crankshaft assembly and rotary valve

1 Piston	9 Crank pin	17 Right-hand bearing	25 Gasket
2 Piston ring	10 Needle bearing	18 Valve plate	26 Screw
3 Gudgeon pin	11 Right-hand flywheel	19 Valve guide	27 Primary drive gear
4 Circlip	12 Left-hand flywheel	20 Guide pin	28 Right-hand oil seal
5 Needle bearing	13 Guide plate	21 Valve seat-outer	29 Spacer
6 Crankshaft assembly	14 Left-hand bearing	22 'O' ring	30 Nut
7 Connecting rod	15 Left-hand spacer	23 Pin	31 Washer
8 Thrust washer	16 Left-hand oil seal	24 Valve seat-inner	32 Key

9 Flywheel generator and stator plate: removal

1 Support the connecting rod using the soft metal bar and two pieces of wood mentioned earlier. Loosen the flywheel nut.
2 Using the Suzuki extractor tool, or a two-leg sprocket puller, loosen the flywheel from the shaft, then remove the nut, flywheel and Woodruff key.
3 Mark the stator plate and casing to assist in assembly and remove the three screws retaining the plate.
4 Disconnect the neutral indicator switch lead from the switch and remove the stator plate.

10 Oil pump: removal

1 Remove the oil pump banjo unions from the pump.
2 Remove the two remaining screws securing the pump.
3 Remove the pump, gasket and plastic drive.
4 Remove the bolt and disconnect the oil supply banjo union to the left-hand crankshaft bearing.
5 Release the oil pipe grommets and remove the oil pipes.

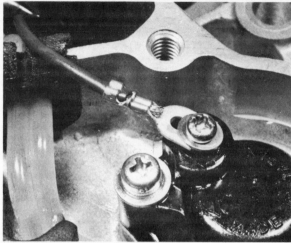

9.4 Disconnect the neutral light switch

10.1 Remove the oil pump banjo unions

10.3a Remove the oil pump, gasket ...

10.3b ... and plastic drive

10.4 Remove the banjo union bolt

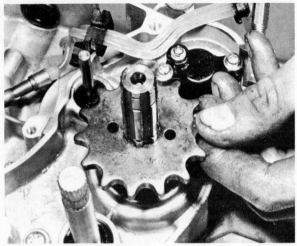

11.1 Draw off the drive sprocket

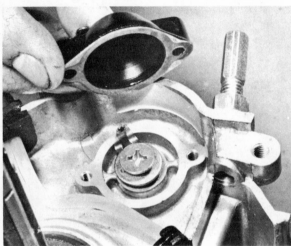

11.2 Remove the neutral light switch cover

11.3 Unscrew the neutral light contact screw

11 Drive sprocket and neutral switch: removal

1   Remove the two spring clips from the drive shaft and pull off the drive sprocket. The A50 mode! has the sprocket secured by a nut and tab washer.
2   Remove the two retaining screws and the neutral switch.
3   Remove the neutral light contact screw and contact.

12 Kickstart spring: removal

1   Remove the two screws from the carburettor casing.
2   Remove a further six screws from the engine casing, on the right-hand side.
3   Remove the right-hand engine casing and remove the gasket if it is not attached to the cover.
4   Release the tang of the kickstart spring. remove the spring and spring guide from the shaft.
5   Remove the circlip and return spring holder.

13 Clutch and primary driven gear: removal

1   Removal of the clutch pressure plate may prove a little difficult as the clutch springs have to be lifted to free their retaining pins. Use a pair of circlip pliers or a hooked piece of stout wire to pull up on the springs to enable the pins to be removed. Care must be taken not to drop the pins into the engine/gearbox.
2   After removing the pins, lift off the pressure plate, followed by the drive and driven plates and the clutch mushroom push piece. Unscrew the springs, if necessary.
3   Lock the engine as previously described. Using a suitable chisel, bend down the locking tab on the clutch sleeve nut lockwasher and remove the nut. Lift out the lockwasher, thrust washer and clutch centre, followed by the clutch outer drum and primary driven gear, thrust washer, spacer, shim and the two clutch push-rods.

14 Primary drive gear: removal

1   Bend down the lockwasher tab and remove the nut.
2   Remove the primary drive gear. Note that the primary gear is located by a Woodruff key.

12.3 Remove the right-hand engine casing

12.4 Release the tang of the kickstart spring

12.5 Remove the circlip and the return spring holder

13.1 Lift to withdraw the spring pins

13.2a Lift off the clutch pressure plate and ...

13.2b ... pull out the clutch mushroom

13.3a Remove the centre nut and ...

13.3b ... pull off the clutch centre

13.3c Remove the clutch outer drum and driven gear ...

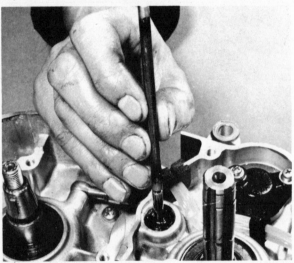

13.3d ... and clutch pushrods.

14.2 Remove the primary drive gear nut

15.1 Remove the linkage, washers and spring

15.2 Pull out the gearchange shaft and lever mechanism

15 Gear selector mechanism: removal

1 Remove the two nuts and washers from the gear selector mechanism and remove the linkage, washers and spring.
2 Remove the gearchange shaft and lever mechanism complete.
3 Remove the selector stopper plate and the four rollers. Note for assembly, the punched hole in the stopper plate goes to the outside and is uppermost.
4 Remove the screw and cam guide.

16 Timing disc and rotary valve: removal

1 Using two stator plate screws and two screwdrivers, ease up and extract the rotary valve cover plate. Remove the O-ring from the cover plate.
2 Remove the rotary valve.
3 Remove five screws and the inner valve seating and gasket.
4 Remove the spacer, rotary valve guide and pin.
Note the exact position of the plate in relation to the shaft, as this positioning is critical to the satisfactory running of the reassembled engine.

15.3 Lift off the selector stopper plate

15.4 Remove the screw and cam guide

16.1 Extract the rotary valve cover plate thus

16.2 Remove the rotary disc, noting its position relative to the shaft

16.3 and the inner valve seating

16.4 Remove the spacer, rotary valve guide and pin

17.2 Carefully separate the crankcase

18.1 Lift out the kickstart pinion assembly

18.2 Pull out the gear selector shaft

17 Separating the crankcase

1   Remove the eight screws. Note the position from which the different length screws are taken, to assist in assembly.
2   Carefully separate the crankcase, removing the left-hand half and leaving all the components in the right-hand half. If the halves are reluctant to part, lightly tap them with a soft-faced mallet to separate them. On no account use a screwdriver to lever them apart as it will inevitably damage the gasket faces. If the crankcase will not part, check that all of the screws have been removed.

18 Crankshaft and gears: removal

1   Remove the kickstart pinion assembly.
2   Remove the gear selector shaft.
3   Remove both gear clusters and the selector drum.
4   Remove the crankshaft assembly.

19 Gears and shaft: separation

1   From the layshaft remove the thrust washer, 5th gear, drive (28 teeth), thrust washer, circlip, split ring, 4th gear, drive (25 teeth), 2nd gear, drive (15 teeth), circlip and 3rd gear, drive (19 teeth).
2   From the main shaft remove the thrust washer, 1st gear, driven (44 teeth), 3rd gear, driven (30 teeth), circlip, 2nd gear, driven (32 teeth), thrust washer, circlip, 4th gear, driven (32 teeth), circlip and 5th gear, driven (30 teeth).
3   If necessary, the gear selector drum may be further dismantled, as shown in Fig. 1.3.

20 Examination and renovation: general

1   Before examining the component part of the dismantled engine/gear unit, it is essential that they should be cleaned thoroughly. Use a paraffin/petrol mix to remove all traces of oil and sludge which may have accumulated within the engine.
2   Use clean, lint-free rags for cleaning and drying the various components, otherwise there is risk of small particles obstructing internal airways.
3   Carefully examine the crankcase castings for cracks or other signs of damage, especially at the mating faces, as damage

here could cause oil leaks. If a crack is discovered, professional attention is required and in an extreme case, renewal of the casting.

4 Examine each part carefully to determine the extent of wear. If in doubt check with the wear and tolerence figures whenever they are quoted in the text. The following Sections will indicate some of the types of wear which can be expected and in many cases, the acceptable limits.

21 Main bearings: renewal

1 Over a long period of use, the main bearings may need to be renewed. It will greatly assist removal and installation of the bearings if the casings are warmed first, in an oven, to approximately 105°C.

2 Having warmed the casings. Carefully press out the right and left-hand crankshaft main bearings.

3 Remove the two screws and retainer and carefully press out the left and right-hand gearbox bearings.

4 Carefully press in the new gearbox bearings, whilst the casings are still warm. Make sure that the bearing outer races are at all times square with the bearing housings. Refit the retainer and the two screws.

5 Oil guide rings are clinched to the crankshaft main bearings. Warm the casing in an oven and press in the bearing assemblies, with the guide ring facing inside the casing and until the guide ring touches the casing.

6 It is sometimes difficult to detect small faults and wear in a bearing. An indication can be obtained by first washing the bearing thoroughly, drying it and lightly lubricating it. Spin the bearing. If it fails to spin freely or if it is noisy, it must be renewed. If in any doubt, always renew as a precautionary measure.

22 Oil seals: removal and examination

1 Old oil seals can be prised out of the crankcase without the use of special tools, if care is taken not to damage the casing. A suitable size of socket can be used. When fitting new oil seals, make sure they are the correct way round. Always pre-lubricate the lips of the oil seals, preferably with a molybdenum disulphide - based grease.

2 It is good policy, if the engine has been stripped completely, to renew all oil seals. Particular attention should be paid to the crankcase oil seals, since if they are worn or damaged they will cause a loss of secondary compression which will result in difficult starting and poor performance.

18.3 Remove both gear clusters and selector drum

18.4 The crankshaft assembly can be lifted out

21.2a The right-hand crankshaft bearing is left in the casing

21.2b The left-hand crankshaft bearing is also left in the casing

23 Gearbox components and kickstart: examination and renovation

1   Examine all the gear pinions, checking for chipped or broken teeth. Also check that the drive dogs are not worn or rounded. Renew as necessary. It is correct practice to always renew gears as a pair, so that they mesh correctly.
2   Check visually that the main and layshafts are not bent.
3   Check the gear selector forks/gear pinion groove clearance renew as necessary.
4   Check that the gear selector forks are not bent or cracked, (particularly near the webbing).
5   Inspect the selector drum tracks for wear. In the unlikely event of excessive wear the drum will have to be renewed.
6   Measure the length of the gear selector shaft release spring. Compare with a new one and renew if necessary.
7   Check the condition of the kickstart ratchet teeth. If they are worn and rounded, the kickstart will slip under load.

24 Clutch components: examination and renovation

1   Measure the full length of the clutch springs and compare with the length of a new spring. Renew as a complete set, if necessary.
2   Measure the thickness of the clutch plates and compare with the Specifications, renew as necessary. Also, check the clutch plates for warping by laying them on a flat surface. Measure the warping with a feeler gauge. Compare with the Specifications and renew as necessary. Inspect the plain plates for scores and renew as required. They are unlikely to wear like the friction plates.
3   Check the clutch plate tongues that locate in the clutch housing are not worn; also examine the smaller teeth that locate with the clutch centre. Any serious indentations or burrs mean new parts will have to be obtained. Small burrs can be removed with an oilstone or a fine cut file. Do not remove too much metal however, since the tongues will then be of unequal width and spacings and consequently will not take up the drive evenly. This unevenness will cause the tongues to wear even more quickly and probably also damage the clutch housing and centre.
4   Examine the clutch centre and housing grooves and dress them if they are not too badly worn. If the grooves made by the plates are left unattended, a sticky clutch action and possibly clutch drag, will result.

25 Decarbonising

1   Remove any build-up of carbon on the piston and/or cylinder head, using wire wool and oil. Any obstinate carbon deposits should be scraped off with a soft metal (aluminium) scraper so as to prevent damage to the head or piston. Do not forget to clean the ports in the cylinder barrel.
2   There will possibly be a ridge of carbon at the top of the cylinder barrel; it is imperative to remove this if a new piston and/or rings are to be fitted.

26 Cylinder head: examination and renovation

1   Clean out any mud and dirt from the fins to prevent over-heating.
2   Check the condition of the thread in the spark plug hole. If it is damaged an effective repair can be made using Helicoil thread insert. This service is available from most Suzuki agents. The cause of a damaged thread can usually be traced to over-tightening of the plug or using a plug of too long a reach. Always use the correct plug and do not overtighten (14.7 lb ft kg m or 22 lb ft as a maximum).
3   Check the cylinder head for warpage (usually caused by uneven tightening and/or over-tightening), with a straight edge across several places on the gasket face; or preferably, with engineers' blue on a surface plate (a sheet of plate glass can be used as a substitute for a surface plate). If the cylinder head is warped, grind it down on a surface plate with emery paper. Start with 200 grade paper and finish with 400 grade and oil.
4   If it is necessary to remove a substantial amount of metal before the cylinder head will seat correctly, a new cylinder head should be obtained.

27 Cylinder barrel and bore: examination and renovation

1   Clean out any mud and dirt from the fins to prevent over-heating.
2   Check the bore for scores. If it is badly marked it will have to be rebored and an oversize piston and rings fitted.
3   Bore wear can be measured using a cylinder bore dial test indicator (or a bore micrometer). If this is unavailable, it is possible to get an idea of the wear by measuring the end gap of a

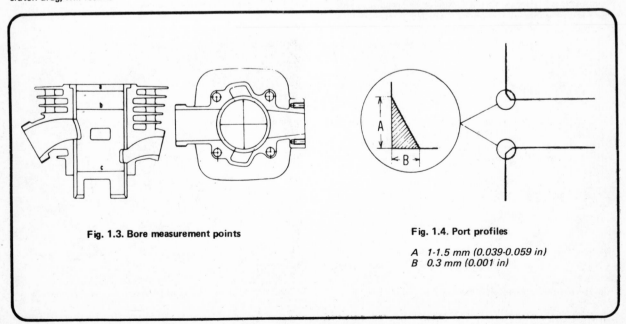

Fig. 1.3. Bore measurement points

Fig. 1.4. Port profiles

A   1-1.5 mm (0.039-0.059 in)
B   0.3 mm (0.001 in)

piston ring placed squarely in the bore at the following three positions: 6 mm (0.24 in) below the cylinder head gasket face, a, 5 mm (0.20 in) above the exhaust port; b, 25 mm (1.0 in) up from the bottom; c, use a set of feeler gauges to measure the end gap. Subtract the smallest measurement from the largest (and divide by three if using the ring method of measurement). If the figures differ by more than 0.05 mm (0.002 in) a rebore is required (see Fig. 1.3).

Note: If the cylinder has been rebored the port edges must be rounded off (top and bottom edges only) to prevent noise and ring wear. Use a file to obtain the measurements given in Fig. 1.4. Finish with 400 grade emery paper. Do not forget to wash the barrel afterwards, to remove all filings and emery dust.

28 Piston and rings: examination and renovation

1   Remove the piston rings by expanding them carefully with the thumbs and lifting the opposite side off the piston. Keep the rings separate so that they can be replaced in the same grooves.
2   The two rings are of the Keystone type ie; tapering inwards on the top surface (see Fig. 1.5). This type of ring is used to help prevent the build-up of carbon and sticking which is a common malaise of two-stroke engines.
3   Check the piston rings by placing each ring in the bottom of the bore (this is the least worn part of the bore). Press it down a little way with the piston to make sure that it is square in the bore. Measure the end gap and compare with the wear limit. Renew if necessary.
4   When fitting new rings always check the end gap and enlarge it, if necessary, by filing with a needle file.
5   Check that the piston and bore are not scored, particularly if the engine has tightened up or seized. If the bore is badly scored, it will require a rebore and oversize piston. If the scoring is not too severe or the piston has just picked up, it is possible to remove the high spots by careful use of a needle file. Do not try to remove the file marks completely, since they will act as oil pockets and assist during the initial bedding in.
6   Before replacing the rings on the piston, make sure that the ring lands are clear of carbon. Be very careful not to damage the lands when cleaning. Also check that the ring locating pegs are not worn. (If they are, a new piston will have to be obtained).
7   The rings are identical when new, but after use will have worn and thus must be replaced in the same piston groove. Ensure that the ring is the correct way up ie; stamped mark facing upwards and that the gaps are positioned over the locating pins.
8   Examine the gudgeon pin for scores or stepped wear, and renew if necessary. Check the gudgeon pin to piston fit, renew if necessary.

29 Small end bearing: examination

1   The small end bearing is of the caged needle roller type, and will seldom give trouble unless a lubrication failure has occurred. The gudgeon pin should be a good sliding fit in the bearing without any play. The bearing must be tested whilst it is in place in the small end eye. If play develops, a noticeable rattle will be heard when the engine is running, indicative of the need for bearing renewal.

30 Piston/bore clearance check

1   Measure the piston diameter 23 mm (0.900 in) above the piston skirt, perpendicular to the gudgeon pin hole.
2   Measure the cylinder bore using an inside micrometer and subtract from this figure the piston diameter obtained in paragraph 1. Compare the result with the Specifications and renew if necessary.
3   Alternatively, if the appropriate measuring equipment is not available, an approximate check of the piston and its bore clearance can be made, using feeler gauges.

31 Engine and gearbox reassembly: general

1   The importance of cleanliness cannot be overstressed. All components must be clean and lightly oiled. All bearings must be pre-lubricated.
2   Renew all gaskets and O-rings. If a gasket or O-ring is unobtainable it is sometimes possible to use one of the modern silicon elastomer products such as Hermetite instant gasket.
3   Remove all traces of old gasket and cement with a solvent such as methylated spirit. It is sometimes convenient to use a little gasket cement to hold a gasket in position when assembling. Use only a good quality, non-setting cement, eg; Golden Hermetite, as required.
4   Ensure all tools are clean. The worst offenders for dirt and grit are sockets and this contamination can easily find its way into an engine.

32 Gears and shafts: reassembly

1   Onto the mainshaft, slide the 5th gear, driven (30 teeth),

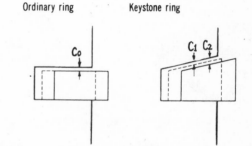

Ordinary ring   Keystone ring

Fig. 1.5. Comparison between Keystone and ordinary piston rings

7° *Taper on top surface of Keystone ring*
Ordinary ring clearance C_o remains constant and allows sticking
Keystone ring clearance changes from C_1 to C_2 and helps to prevent sticking

32.1a The layshaft 5th gear, pinion and circlip

32.1b Follow with 4th gear pinion, circlip, washer and ...

32.1c ... then 2nd gear pinion and circlip ...

32.1d ... 3rd gear pinion with selector groove ...

32.1e ... 1st gear pinion and thrust washer last

32.2a Slide the mainshaft 1st gear on shaft and fit circlip, then ...

32.2b ... fit 2nd and 4th gear pinions, followed by ...

32.2c ... split ring and ...

32.2d ... circlip and thrust washer and ...

32.2e ... 5th gear pinion and thrust washer

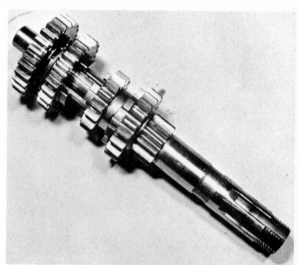

32.2f The complete layshaft assembly

32.3a Do not forget to fit pawl pin with rounded end outwards

32.3b Insert in kickstart drive pinion

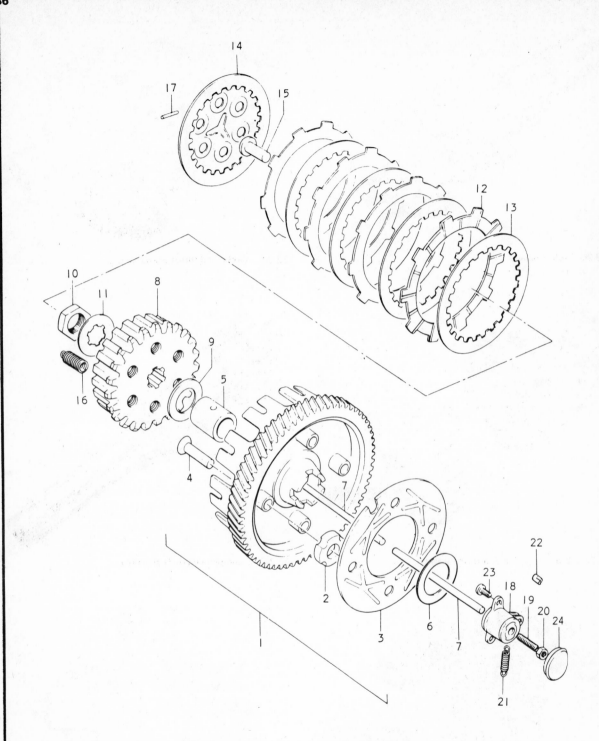

Fig. 1.6. Clutch assembly

1 Primary driven gear	7 Pushrod	13 Plate - driven	19 Screw adjuster
2 Damper	8 Hub sleeve	14 Plate - pressure	20 Nut
3 Plate	9 Thrust washer	15 Clutch push piece	21 Spring
4 Rivet	10 Nut	16 Spring	22 End piece
5 Spacer	11 Lockwasher	17 Pin	23 Screw
6 Thrust washer	12 Plate - drive	18 Screw assembly	24 Cap

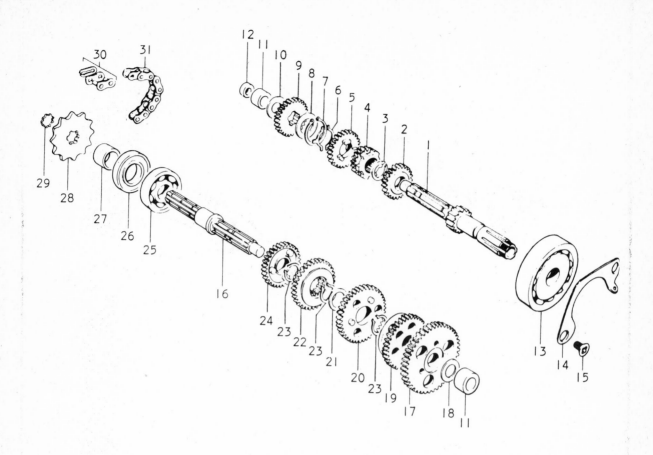

Fig. 1.7. Gearbox components

1	Mainshaft	9	5th gear - mainshaft
2	3rd gear - mainshaft	10	Thrust washer
3	Circlip	11	Bush
4	2nd gear - mainshaft	12	Oil seal
5	4th gear - mainshaft	13	Right-hand bearing
6	Knock ring	14	Retainer
7	Circlip	15	Screw
8	Thrust washer	16	Layshaft

17	1st gear - layshaft	25	Bearing
18	Thrust washer	26	Oil seal
19	3rd gear - layshaft	27	Bush
20	2nd gear - layshaft	28	Engine sprocket
21	Thrust washer	29	Ring
22	4th gear - layshaft	30	Spring link
23	Circlip	31	Final drive chain
24	5th gear - layshaft		

circlip, 4th gear driven (32 teeth), circlip, thrust washer, 2nd gear driven (32 teeth) circlip, 3rd gear driven (30 teeth), 1st gear driven (44 teeth) and thrust washer.

2 Onto the layshaft slide the 3rd gear driver (19 teeth), circlip, 2nd gear driver (15 teeth), 4th gear driver (25 teeth), split ring, circlip, thrust washer, 5th gear driver (28 teeth) and thrust washer.

3 Fit the thrust washer to the kickstart shaft, followed by the pawl spring, pawl pin - with its rounded end outwards, and the pawl. While holding the assembly together, fit the drive gear. Line up the punch marks on the drive gear with those in the valley of one of the shaft splines.

4 Check that the pawl is correctly positioned by holding the shaft and turning the drive gear. The pawl should engage and lock. When turned the other way it should have a ratchet action.

33 Crankshaft assembly: installation

1 Install the crankshaft assembly into the crankcase. Do not forget the crankshaft spacer.

34 Gear cluster and selector: reassembly

1 Assemble the selector forks onto the drum and fit the locating pins. Fit new split pins with their closed ends facing inwards. If fitted the other way round there is a chance of them fouling.

2 Assemble the gear cluster and selector drum as a whole and fit them into the crankcase, followed by the kickstart shaft assembly.

3 Fit the gearchange fork and shaft assembly.

35 Crankcase: assembly

1 Check that the crankcase mating faces are clean and flat and that the two locating dowels are in position. Fit a new gasket and carefully assemble the two halves of the crankcase together, locating the gear shafts into position. Do not use undue force.

2 Fit two or three of the crankcase screws and check that the crankshaft and gearshafts all rotate freely; if not, remove the

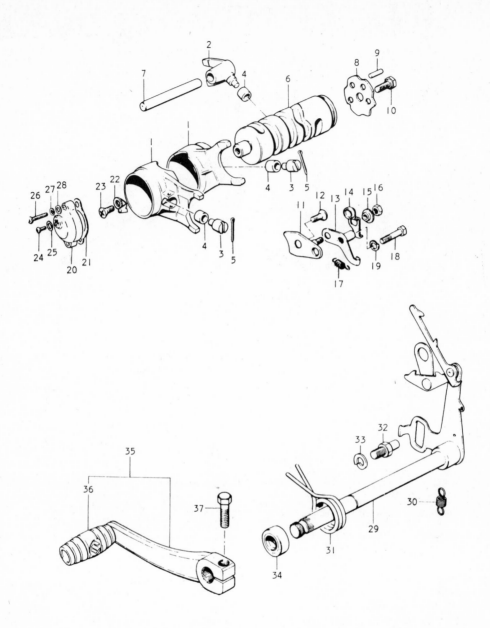

Fig. 1.8. Gear selector mechanism

1	Fork - low speed	10	Bolt	19	Lockwasher	28	Washer
2	Fork - high speed	11	Guide	20	Switch body	29	Shaft
3	Guide	12	Screw	21	Gasket	30	Spring - pawl return
4	Roller	13	Holder	22	Contact, neutral switch	31	Spring - shaft return
5	Split pin	14	Stopper	23	Screw	32	Stopper
6	Cam	15	Spacer	24	Screw	33	Lockwasher
7	Shaft	16	Nut	25	Washer	34	Oil seal
8	Stopper plate	17	Spring	26	Screw	35	Lever assembly
9	Pin	18	Bolt	27	Lockwasher	36	Rubber
						37	Bolt

33.1 Do not forget the camshaft spacer

34.2a Assemble the gear cluster ...

34.2b .. and the selector drum as a whole unit ...

34.2c ... and fit them into the crankcase ...

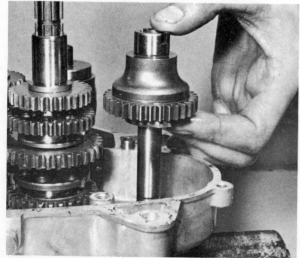

34.2d ... followed by the kickstart shaft assembly

34.3 Fit the gearchange fork and shaft assembly

36.1a Replace the gearchange cam guide ...

36.1b ... followed by the stopper plate and four pins

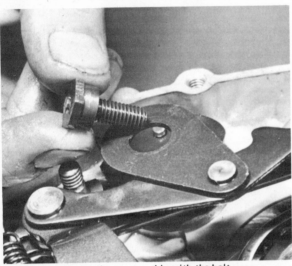

36.2 Secure the gearchange assembly with the bolt

36.3a Replace the gearchange cam stopper and spring ...

36.3b ... and secure with the nut and bolt

37.1 Fit the inner rotary valve seating.

37.2a Replace the pin in the crankshaft and ...

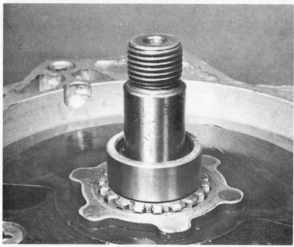

37.2b ... the valve guide, valve plate and spacer

37.2c Punch marks must align with crankshaft keyway ...

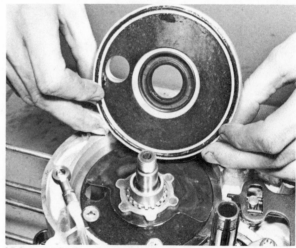

37.3 ... and fit the valve cover plate

37.4 Locate the positioning dowel

screws and check that everything has been assembled correctly.
3   On satisfactory completion of the foregoing operation, fit the remainder of the crankcase screws. Tighten down evenly and in a diagonal sequence, until all are tight. Re-check that all shafts still revolve quite freely.

36 Selector mechanism: reassembly

1   Fit the gearchange cam guide and locking screw, followed by the stopper plate and four pins. The punched hole in the stopper plate is fitted to the outside and is uppermost, for correct assembly.
2   Fit the lever mechanism and gearchange shaft complete and secure with the bolt.
3   Fit the gearchange cam stopper and spring, and secure with the nut and bolt.

37 Timing disc and rotary valve: reassembly

1   Fit the gasket and inner valve seat. Secure with the five screws.
2   Fit the pin to the crankshaft and fit the valve guide, valve plate, and spacer. Ensure the punched dots are aligned with the

keyway in the crankshaft.
3   Lightly grease the O-ring and fit it to the valve cover plate.
4   Lightly oil the cover plate seal, locate the positioning dowel and fit the cover plate, tapping it gently into place.

38 Primary drive gear: reassembly

1   Fit the Woodruff key to the crankshaft and fit the drive pinion to locate with the Woodruff key.
2   Fit the washer and nut. Using two pieces of wood and suitable bolt, support the connecting rod as previously described, and tighten the drive pinion nut to 5.0 kg f m (36 lb f ft).
3   Using a suitable chisel, lock the nut by bending the lockwasher tab.

39 Clutch: reassembly

1   Fit the thrust washer and spacer to the gearshaft followed by the clutch outer drum and primary pinion, to mesh with the drive pinion.

38.1 Do not forget to fit the Woodruff key

38.2 Fit the retaining washer and nut

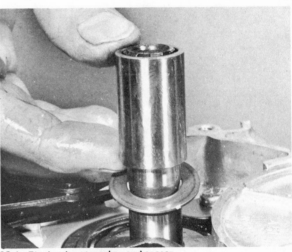

39.1a Fit the thrust washer and spacer ...

39.1b ... followed by the clutch outer drum and primary gear

39.2a Fit the thrust washer ...

2   Fit the thrust washer and clutch centre assembly, having first installed the springs.

3   Fit the lockwasher and nut. Tighten the nut to 5.0 kg f m (36 lb f ft) torque and lock the nut by bending up the lockwasher. Support the clutch hub and pinion gear when tightening the nut.

4   Fit the clutch mushroom push piece followed by a driven plate and drive plate, four of each in that order, in the reverse of removal.

5   Fit the pressure plate and align the positioning marks. Using suitable tools, such as long-nosed pliers and circlip pliers, pull up on each spring and fit the spring pins.

40 Kickstart spring: reassembly

1   Fit the kickstart return spring holder and circlip, followed by the kickstart spring. Locate the lower end of the spring in the hole provided for it in the casing. Turn the kickstart shaft fully clockwise, twist the spring anticlockwise about half a turn and insert the upper tang of the spring into the hole provided for it in the shaft.

2   Fit the plastic spring guide.

39.2b ... and the clutch centre assembly

39.4a Fit the clutch mushroom and ...

39.4b ... the clutch plates, four of each in order

39.5a Fit the pressure plate and ...

39.5b ... insert the pins through the spring ends

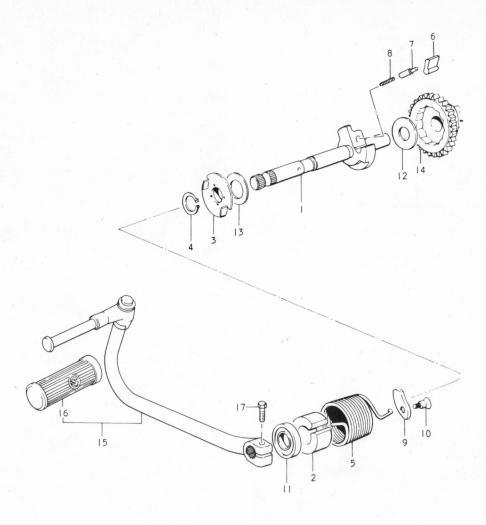

Fig. 1.9. Kickstart

1	Shaft	5	Spring	9	Stopper	13	Thrust washer - RH
2	Guide	6	Pawl	10	Screw	14	Drive gear
3	Holder	7	Pin	11	Oil seal	15	Lever assembly
4	Circlip	8	Spring	12	Thrust washer - LH	16	Rubber
						17	Bolt

41 Right-hand engine cover: installation

1   Make sure that the mating faces are clean and undamaged. Check that the two locating dowels are in position and fit a new gasket.
2   Position the main bearing oil pipe in its locating grommets and screw the oil pipe banjo connection with the union bolt. Make sure there is a sealing washer fitted each side of the banjo union.
3   Carefully position and fit the cover, securing it with the ten screws.

42 Neutral light assembly and clutch push-rods: installation

1   Fit the neutral light contact and screw, locating the contact lug to ensure the correct location.

2   Fit the neutral light switch and gasket, with the contact screw uppermost.
3   Fit both clutch push-rods.

43 Oil pump and cover: installation

1   Fit the oil pump driving piece (white plastic), and gasket.
2   Install the oil pump and ensure that the driving piece locates correctly into the pump. Secure the pump with the two screws and tighten them evenly.
3   Using a pressure oil can filled with two-stroke oil, prime the pump and both oil pipes.
4   Make sure there are sealing washers between the pipe banjo union connections and the pump and secure the oil pipes to the pump with the bolts and washers.
5   Locate the oil pipes in their respective rubber grommets.

40.1a Replace the kickstart return spring holder and circlip

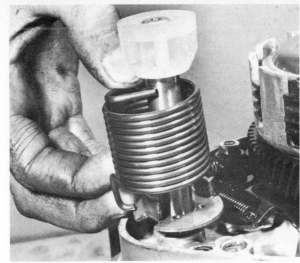

40.1b Locate the lower end of the spring correctly

40.2 Fit the plastic spring guide

42.1 Fit the neutral light switch cover

43.1 Make sure the oil pump driving piece locates correctly

43.4 Secure the oil pipes to the pump body

43.6 Fit the engine feed pipe union

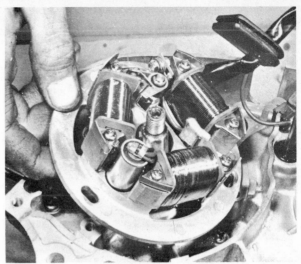
44.1a Position the stator plate assembly and ...

44.1b ... align the centre punch marks made earlier

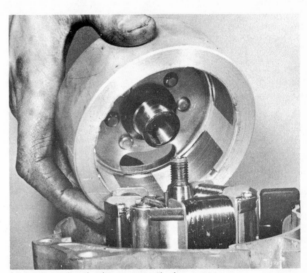
44.3 Fit the flywheel rotor over the key

45.1 Secure the gearbox sprocket with the two spring clips

47.3 Lubricate the small end bearing

6   Make sure there is a sealing washer between the pipe banjo
union connection and the left-hand bearing bolt hole. Fit the
pipe union securing it with the bolt and washer.
7   Fit the oil pump cover and secure it with the retaining screw.

44 Flywheel, stator plate and neutral light switch lead: reassembly

1   Position the stator plate assembly and secure with the three
screws. Before final tightening, align the centre punch marks,
made during dismantling. If no marks were made, position the
stator plate screw slots approximately midway and tighten the
screws.
2   Secure the neutral light switch lead to the switch.
3   Fit the Woodruff key into its keyway on the shaft and make
sure the tapers on the shaft and in the flywheel are clean and
free of grease. Fit the flywheel and secure it with the washer,
spring washer and nut.
4   Check the contact breaker points gap and the ignition timing.
See Chapter 3, Sections 5 and 6.
5   Tighten the flywheel nut to 3.5 - 4.5 kg f m (25 - 33 lb f ft)
supporting the crankshaft and connecting rod as previously
described.

45 Final drive sprocket: installation

1   Fit the final drive sprocket to the gearbox shaft and secure
it with the two spring clips or the nut and tab washer (A50M).

46 Left-hand cover: installation

Fit the left-hand cover gasket and cover. Secure it with the
six screws temporarily, until the unit is installed in the frame.

47 Cylinder barrel, piston and cylinder head: assembly

1   Ensure the mating faces of all components are clean and dry.
2   Fit a new cylinder base gasket and lubricate the big end
bearing with a little two-stroke oil. Do NOT use gasket cement
at this joint.
3   Lubricate the small end needle bearing and fit to the
connecting rod.
4   Fit the piston and rings, with the arrow on the piston crown
facing towards the exhaust port. Fit the gudgeon pin and secure
it with the two new circlips, making sure they have seated
properly in their grooves. It is bad policy to use old circlips as
they have lost much of their spring tension and may jump out
and cause the engine to seize.
5   Remove any rag from around the connecting rod, lubricate
the piston, rings and bore of the cylinder barrel. Align the
piston ring gaps over their locating pegs and slide the cylinder
barrel over the piston and down over the holding down studs,
whilst compressing the piston rings with the fingers to assist
assembly.
6   When the cylinder barrel is seated correctly, fit a new
aluminium cylinder head gasket. Do NOT use any gasket
cement at this joint.
7   Fit the cylinder head, with the plug, or plug hole, uppermost.
Secure the cylinder head with the four washers and nuts. Torque
tighten the nuts to 100 kg cm (7.2 ft lb) in a diagonal
sequence. Squirt a little two-stroke oil into the plug hole and
turn the engine over a few times.

48 Fitting the engine/gearbox into the frame

1   The engine/gearbox can now be installed into the frame by
reversing the removal procedure given in Section 3 of this Chapter.
Always fit a new exhaust gasket before replacing the exhaust

47.4a Fit the piston and rings ...

47.4b ... with the arrow on the piston crown facing the front

47.5a Align the piston ring gaps with the pegs

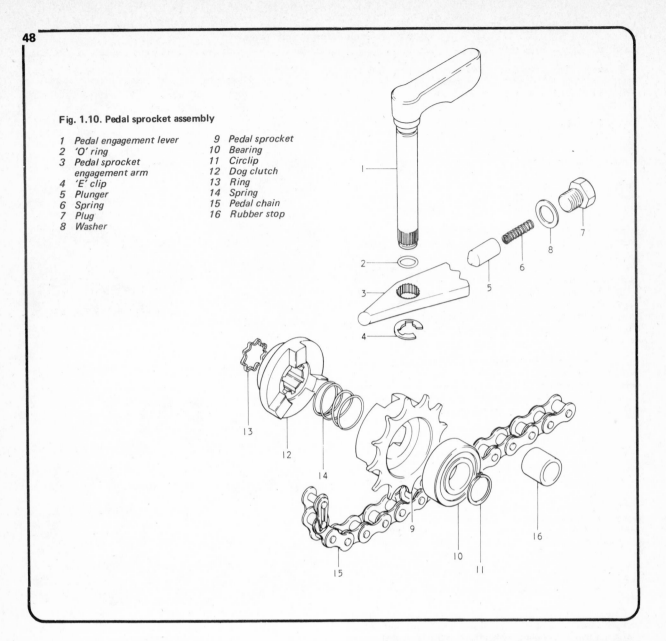

Fig. 1.10. Pedal sprocket assembly

1	Pedal engagement lever	9	Pedal sprocket
2	'O' ring	10	Bearing
3	Pedal sprocket engagement arm	11	Circlip
4	'E' clip	12	Dog clutch
5	Plunger	13	Ring
6	Spring	14	Spring
7	Plug	15	Pedal chain
8	Washer	16	Rubber stop

47.5b Slide the cylinder barrel over the piston

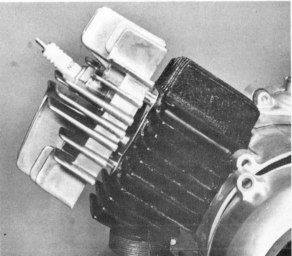

47.7 Fit the cylinder head, using a new gasket

system.

2 When fitting the kickstart and gear levers, use a little thread locking compound eg; Torqueseal, on the pinch bolts; this prevents the levers from working loose and thereby damaging the splines.

49 Final operations and adjustments

1 If the spark plug has not been fitted, it must be gapped to 0.6 - 0.7 mm (0.024 - 0.028 in) and fitted to the cylinder head. Do not overtighten.

2 Refill the transmission with 550 cc (1.0 pint) of clean oil of the recommended viscosity.

3 Adjust the clutch by slackening the adjuster locknut and turning the screw until it touches the push-rod. Back out the screw half a turn and tighten the locknut.

4 Check the oil pump adjustment and adjust, if necessary. Make sure the oil pump is primed with oil by means of the bleed screw.

50 Starting and running the rebuilt engine

1 When the initial start-up is made, run the engine slowly for the first few minutes, especially if the engine has been rebored or a new crankshaft fitted. Check that all the controls function correctly and that there are no oil leaks before taking the machine on the road. The exhaust will emit a high proportion of white smoke during the first few miles, as the excess oil used whilst the engine was reassembled is burnt away. The volume of smoke should gradually diminish until only the customary light blue haze is observed during normal running. It is wise to carry a spare spark plug during the first run, since the existing plug may oil up due to the temporary excess of oil.

2 Remember that a good seal between the pistons and the cylinder barrels is essential for the correct functioning of the engine. A rebored two-stroke engine will require more careful running-in, over a long period, than its four-stroke counterpart. There is a far greater risk of engine seizure during the first hundred miles if the engine is permitted to work hard.

3 Do not tamper with the exhaust system or run the engine without the baffle fitted to the silencer. Unwarranted changes in the exhaust system will have a very marked effect on engine performance, invariably for the worst. The same advice to dispensing with the air cleaner or the air cleaner element.

4 Do not on any account add oil to the petrol under the mistaken belief that a little extra oil will improve the engine lubrication. Apart from creating excess smoke, the addition of oil will make the mixture much weaker, with the consequent risk of overheating and engine seizure. The oil pump alone should provide full engine lubrication.

51 Fault diagnosis: engine

Symptom	Cause	Remedy
Engine will not start	Defective spark plug	Remove plug and lay on cylinder head. Check whether spark occurs when engine is kicked over.
	Dirty or closed contact breaker points	Check condition of points and whether gap is correct.
	Air leak at crankcase or worn crankshaft oil seals	Check whether petrol is reaching the spark plug.
Engine runs unevenly	Ignition and/or fuel system fault	Check systems independently as though engine will not start.
	Blowing cylinder head gasket	Leak should be evident from oil leakage where gas escapes.
	Incorrect ignition timing	Check timing very accurately and reset if necessary.
Lack of power	Fault in fuel system or incorrect ignition timing	See above.
	Choked silencer	Remove and clean out baffles.
High fuel/oil consumption	Cylinder barrel in need of rebore and o/s piston	Fit new rings and piston after rebore.
	Oil leaks or air leaks from damaged gaskets or oil seals	Trace source of leak and replace damaged gasket and/or seal.
Excessive mechanical noise	Worn cylinder barrel (piston slap)	Rebore and fit o/s piston.
	Worn small end bearings (rattle)	Replace needle roller bearing (caged) and if necessary, gudgeon pin.
	Worn big end bearing (knock)	Fit replacement crankshaft assembly.
	Worn main bearings (rumble)	Fit new journal bearings and seals.
Engine overheats and fades	Pre-ignition and/or weak mixture	Check carburettor settings. Check also whether plug grade is correct.
	Lubrication failure	Check oil pump setting and whether oil tank is empty.

52 Fault diagnosis: clutch

Symptom	Cause	Remedy
Engine speed increases but machine does not respond	Clutch slip	Check clutch adjustment for free play at handlebar lever. Check condition of clutch plate linings, also whether clutch spring bolts are tight.
Difficulty in engaging gears. Gear changes jerky and machine creeps forward, even when clutch is withdrawn. Difficulty in selecting neutral	Clutch drag	Check clutch adjustment for too much free play. Check for burrs on clutch plate tongues or indentations in clutch drum slots. Dress with file if damage not too great.
	Clutch assembly loose on mainshaft	Check tightness of retaining nut. If loose, fit new tab washer and retighten.
Operation action stiff	Damaged, trapped or frayed control cable	Check cable and replace if necessary. Make sure cable is lubricated and has no sharp bends.
	Bent pushrod(s)	Renew.

53 Fault diagnosis: gearbox

Symptom	Cause	Remedy
Difficulty in engaging gears	Gear selector forks bent	Renew.
	Gear cluster assembled incorrectly	Check that thrust washers are located correctly.
Machine jumps out of gear	Worn dogs on ends of gear pinions	Renew pinions involved.
	Selector drum pawls stuck	Free pawl assembly.
Gear lever does not return to normal position	Broken return spring	Renew spring.
Kickstart does not return when engine is turned over or started	Broken or poorly tensioned return spring	Renew spring or retension.
Kickstart slips	Kickstart drive pinion internals, pawls or springs worn badly	Renew all worn parts.

Chapter 2 Fuel system and Lubrication

Contents

Specifications

Carburettors

Type	VM16SC
Main jet	72.5
Throttle needle	3G - 2 3GI - 3 (A50)
Needle jet	E - 2
Throttle slide cutaway	CA : 2.0
Pilot jet ... ...·	25
Pilot air adjusting screw	1½ turns
Cold start jet	40
Pilot jet outlet	0.9 mm
Needle valve seat	1.2 mm
Float height (above gasket face)	22.5 mm (0.89 in) with gasket removed

1 The fuel system: general description

Fuel from the petrol tank is fed via a tap having an integral filter, to the float chamber of the VM16SC carburettor. The carburettor is of the fixed choke type with a cylindrical throttle slide. A cable operated, cold starting facility is provided. The air is cleaned by a resin - processed paper filter located on the frame.

2 Seat and petrol tank: removal and replacement

1 To remove the seat, unscrew the two bolts, washers and spring washers securing the rear of the seat and gently pull the front part off the frame bracket.
2 Remove the petrol tank, disconnect the petrol pipe from the petrol tap.

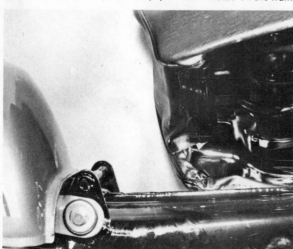

2.1a Remove the two bolts at the rear of the seat

2.1b Pull the front part off

2.3 Remove the two bolts and washers that retain the tank

3.1 Check the condition of the 'O' ring seal

3.3 Carefully guide stems out of the tank

3 Remove the two bolts, and washers securing the tank to the frame and gently pull the front of the tank from the two round cushions.
4 Check the tank for splits and leaks. Also check the condition of the support cushions.
5 Replace the tank and seat by reversing the removal procedure.

3 Fuel tap

1 The sediment bowl of the fuel tap should be cleaned out periodically. It is removed by unscrewing. When refitting, check that the upper securing bolts are not loose and leaking. Tighten as necessary. Also, check the O-ring seal.
2 If the fuel tap is leaking, it is most likely due to damage or deterioration of the rubber seals. To gain access to them remove the two screws from the lever retaining plate. Lift off the plate and O-ring and pull out the tap lever. If necessary, renew the rubber seals. The tank must be drained of fuel for this operation.
3 The fuel tap is removed by taking out the two bolts and washers and carefully guiding the tap stems from out of the tank. The tank must be drained for this operation. Replacement is the reverse of removal.

4 Carburettor: dismantling, examination and assembly

1 To remove the carburettor, detach the right-hand side access panel, and remove the retaining screws securing the carburettor cover. Ease the cover up the cables and unscrew both the cold start device and the top that retains the slide assembly of the carburettor.
2 Using a screwdriver, loosen the bolt securing the carburettor to the cylinder flange and remove the carburettor.
3 Remove the four screws and lift off the float bowl which will uncover the jets and float. Remove the drain plug.
4 Slide out the pivot pin and lift off the float. The needle valve seat is now free to be removed.
5 Remove the pilot jet, followed by the needle jet and the needle valve assembly. Note the copper washer. The main jet can be removed from the needle jet, if necessary. If required, remove the air screw and spring, noting the setting by counting the number of turns required to remove it.
6 The cold start plunger and adjuster can be removed from the cable by sliding it off sideways.

4.1 Ease up the cover

4.3. Lift off the float bowl

4.4a Slide out the pivot pin

4.4b The needle valve is now free

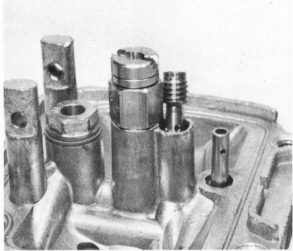
4.5a Remove the pilot jet ...

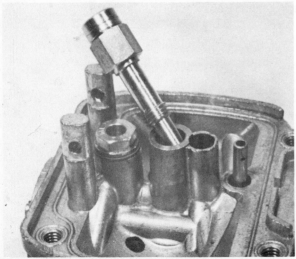
4.5b ... followed by the needle jet

4.5c ... and the needle valve assembly

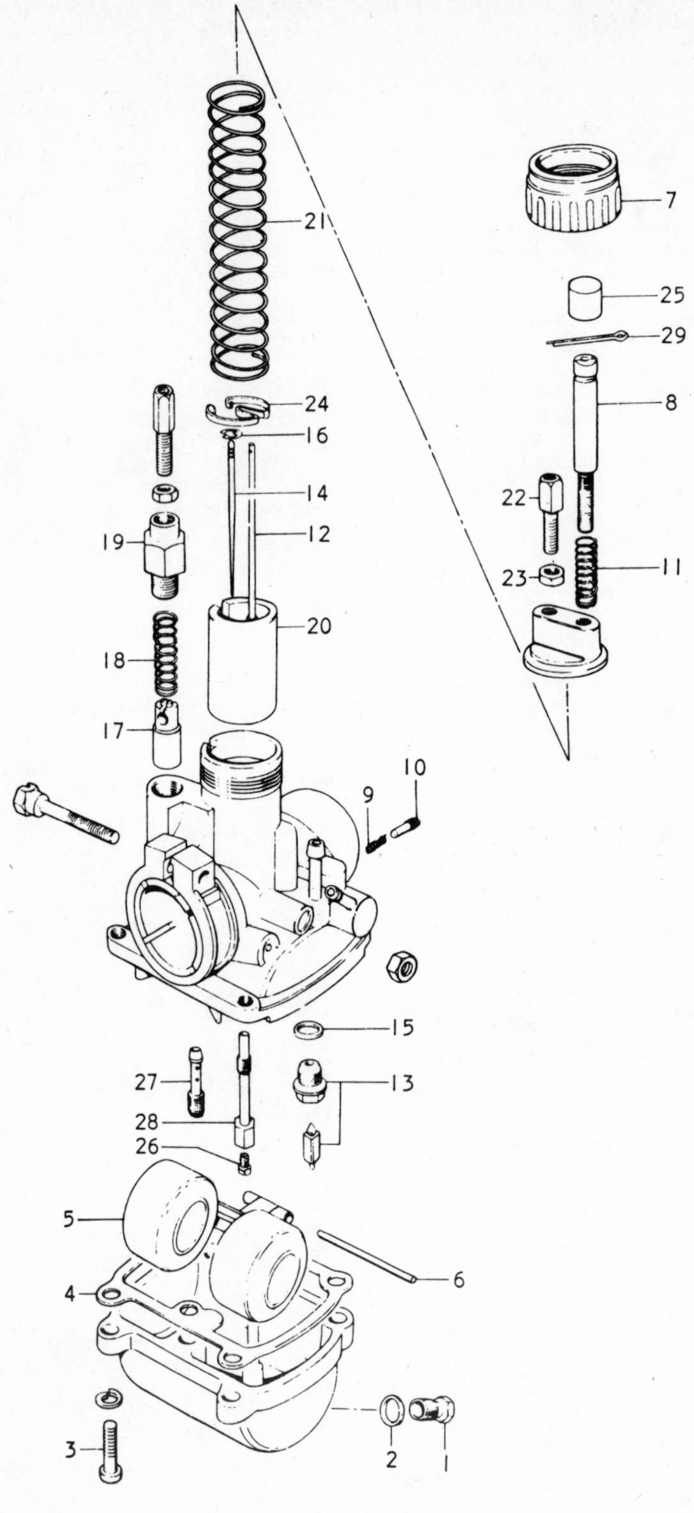

Fig. 2.1. Carburettor

1	Drain plug	8	Screw - throttle valve stop	15	Gasket	22	Adjuster
2	Gasket	9	Spring	16	Needle clip	23	Nut
3	Screw	10	Screw - air	17	Plunger	24	Seat
4	Gasket	11	Spring	18	Spring	25	Cap
5	Float	12	Rod	19	Cap	26	Jet - main
6	Pin	13	Needle valve assembly	20	Valve - throttle	27	Jet - pilot
7	Cap	14	Needle	21	Spring - throttle	28	Jet - needle
						29	Split pin

7   The throttle slide is a little unusual since it also includes a throttle stop device. Remove the throttle stop split pin; this frees the rod. Remove the throttle cable by pushing the cable down the slide and moving the nipple to one side. The needle is held in the slide by a seat and spring clip. Pull the former out and remove the needle. The needle is held in position by a circlip in one of its five grooves. Note which groove holds the circlip.

8   Check that the needle is not bent by rolling it on a flat surface. If it has worn, obtain a new replacement and also renew the needle jet.

9   Check that the throttle slide is not worn or scored. Renew as necessary. If the throttle slide is badly scored, check also the condition of the carburettor body, which may also require renewal.

10 Do not use wire or any other thin metal object to clear a blocked jet. The hole can easily become enlarged or mishapen, which will seriously affect the flow of fuel. To clean the jets, blow them out with compressed air, eg; a foot pump.

11 Check the float assembly for leaks by shaking it. If petrol can be heard inside a float a new one will be required. Check the float height by measuring the distance from the gasket face to the bottom of the float assembly. The float tongue must be just touching the float needle when measuring. If necessary, bend the tongue to obtain the correct 20.5 mm (0.81 in) setting.

12 To assemble the carburettor, reverse the above procedure. Do not overtighten the jet and renew the gasket, if damaged.

5 Carburettor: adjustment

1   All adjustments should be made when the engine is at its normal working temperature and the machine is standing on level ground.

2   Screw the pilot jet fully home and then unscrew it 1½ turns for the A50 and A50P models and 2 full turns for the AS50 model. Screwing the adjuster further out weakens the mixture and vice versa. Set the needle clip in the fourth groove from the top.

3   With the engine running adjust the throttle stop rod (on top of the carburettor) for a fast tick-over.

4   Adjust the pilot air adjuster screw, if necessary, until the engine runs smoothly without hunting or misfiring.

5   Reduce the engine speed at the throttle stop rod. Do not arrive at a setting where the engine runs too slowly, otherwise there is a risk of stalling when the throttle is closed. Note that by virtue of its design, a two-stroke engine will not run evenly at very low engine speeds.

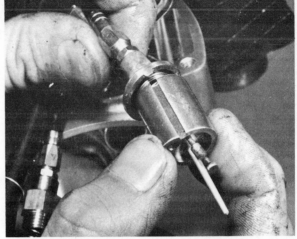
4.7a To release the slide, push the cable downwards

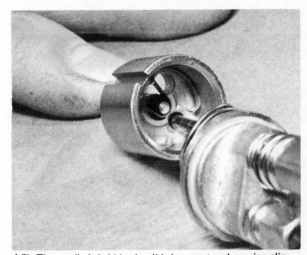
4.7b The needle is held in the slide by a seat and a spring clip

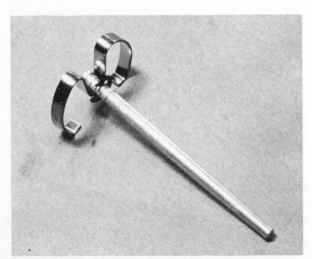
4.7c Note which groove holds the circlip

5.2 Unscrew 1½ turns for the A50 and A50P models

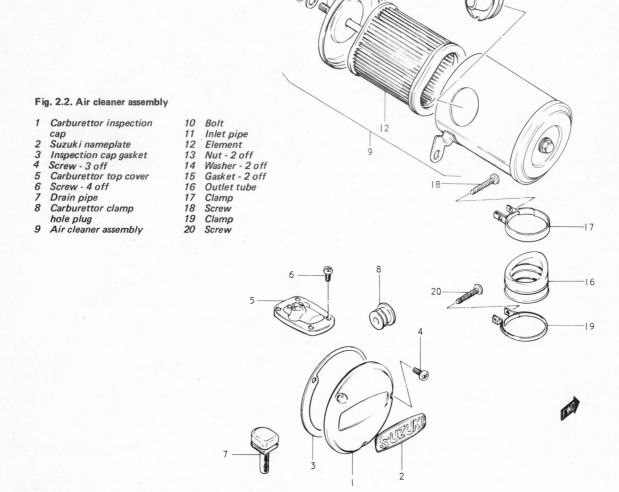

Fig. 2.2. Air cleaner assembly

1	Carburettor inspection cap	10	Bolt
2	Suzuki nameplate	11	Inlet pipe
3	Inspection cap gasket	12	Element
4	Screw - 3 off	13	Nut - 2 off
5	Carburettor top cover	14	Washer - 2 off
6	Screw - 4 off	15	Gasket - 2 off
7	Drain pipe	16	Outlet tube
8	Carburettor clamp hole plug	17	Clamp
		18	Screw
9	Air cleaner assembly	19	Clamp
		20	Screw

6.2 Remove the end cap and bolt

6   Adjust the throttle cable free play to 0.5 - 1.0 mm (0.020 - 0.040 in) by turning the cable adjuster of the twist grip. There should be approximately 0.5 mm (0.020 in) play at full throttle.
7   The amount of slide cutaway, sizes of main jet, needle jet and pilot jet are predetermined for optimum running by the manufacturer and should not require any variation.
8   The pilot jet controls engine speeds up to approximately 1/8 throttle and the degrees of the throttle slide cutaway from 1/8 to ¼ throttle. Thereafter the needle jet takes over up to ¾ throttle. The main jet controls the final ¾ to full throttle. There stages are only approximate since there is a certain amount of overlap.

6   Air cleaner: location and cleaning

1   The air cleaner is located above the engine/gearbox unit and the casing is secured by a rubber grommet and spring clip.
2   To remove the filter element, unscrew the domed nut, take off the washer and remove the end cap and bolt from the casing. This will expose the filter element.
3   Clean the element by tapping it sharply several times.

Alternatively, if available, use a low pressure air line and blow from the inside of the element. On no account wash the element or allow it to become wet since it will become permanently damaged.

4 If the filter element is very dirty or the machine is used in dusty conditions, the element should be renewed.

5 It is bad practice to use the machine with a damaged element or without one, since this will weaken the mixture and may cause over-heating and possible seizure.

7 Lubrication system: general description

1 Lubrication consists of two separate systems, one for the crankshaft and engine internals (the Suzuki CCI system) and the other for the transmission.

2 The CCI system consists of an oil tank which gravity feeds a variable rate pump with oil of the correct viscosity (SAE30). The pump is driven from the left-hand side of the gearbox. The oil is fed from the pump to the left and right-hand main bearings and from there to the big-end bearing. The oil then escapes into the crankcase and mixes with the petrol to form a fine mist which in turn lubricates the piston and small end bearing. The pump discharge rate is controlled by the throttle opening and therefore the amount of oil is regulated to that required by the engine. This system is far more economical and free from the inherent problems of the old petrol/oil mixtures lubrication that was at one time commonplace for two-strokes.

3 The transmission is lubricated by the wet sump method and the oil requires only routine checking and changing at the recommended intervals.

8 Oil pump: dismantling

It is unlikely that the pump will require any attention due to the very low rate of wear. Also, due to the precision fit of the components, it is not recommended that the pump be dismantled.

9 Oil tank: removal and installation

1 The oil tank should not require any attention unless it is damaged in an accident. It is secured at the rear by three bolts and washers.

2 If the sight lens requires cleaning or renewal, it is secured by the central crosshead screw. The tank must be drained of oil first.

3 An oil filter is fitted in the union joint nut and should be periodically cleaned. Drain the tank by unscrewing the union bolt and then remove the union joint nut which will expose the filter. Clean the filter in petrol.

4 To bleed the pipe after refitting the tank, fill the tank, then slacken the union bolt until oil flows out. Retighten the bolt. The system must ALWAYS be bled of air whenever it is disturbed.

5 Periodically check that the breather pipe is clear and not blocked.

10 Oil pump: bleeding

1 If the oil pump feed pipes have leaks or if the pump has been removed, it is important to bleed the pump.

2 Ensure that the oil tank contains a plentiful supply of two-stroke or SAE 30 oil.

3 Slacken off the union bolt of the inlet pipe to the top of the pump and check there is an air-free flow of oil to the pump. Tighten the union bolt.

4 Remove the two outlet union bolts in turn and pressure prime the main bearing lines. Reconnect and tighten the pump outlet unions.

5 Start the engine and at a fast tick-over, move the pump operating lever over to maximum and check that there are no air bubbles in the outlet pipes. Release the lever and stop the engine when satisfied all air has been removed.

11 Oil pump cable: adjustment

1 The oil pump cable adjustment must be checked after adjusting the carburettor cables.

2 Loosen the adjuster locknut and fully open the throttle.

3 Turn the adjuster until the marks on the control lever and pump body are aligned correctly. When these marks are in register the top section of the dot mark on the carburettor slide should be aligned with the top of the carburettor bore.

4 Tighten the adjuster locknut.

12 Silencer: decarbonising

1 The silencer of a two-stroke is very prone to becoming

12.2 Baffle is retained by one crosshead screw

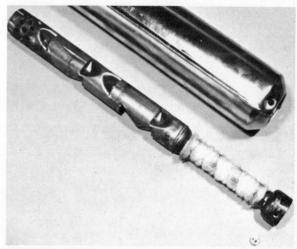

12.3 Make sure all the holes are clear

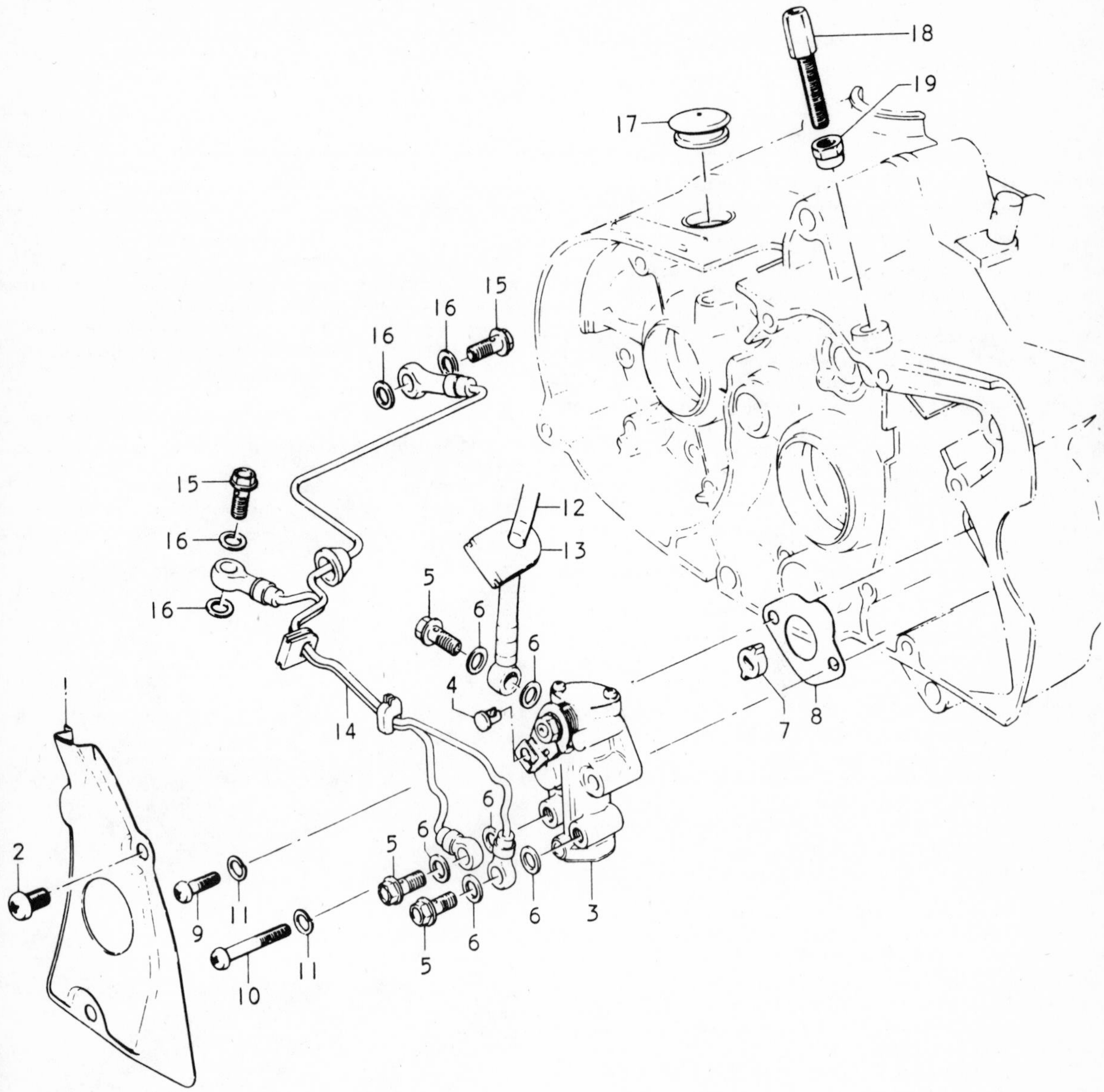

Fig. 2.3. Oil pump

1	Cover	6	Gasket	11	Lockwasher	16	Gasket
2	Screw	7	Driving piece	12	Hose - inlet	17	Cap
3	Pump	8	Gasket	13	Grommet	18	Adjuster
4	Trunnion	9	Screw	14	Hose - outlet	19	Nut
5	Union bolt	10	Screw	15	Bolt		

blocked with carbon deposits, which leads to a general lack of performance and eventually bad starting.

2   The silencer is fitted with a removable baffle, retained by one crosshead screw. The baffle can be difficult to remove, especially if it is badly caked up.

3   Scrape out as much carbon as possible, both from the silencer and baffle, making sure all the holes are clear.

4   Refit the baffle and tighten the screw. Never run the machine without a baffle fitted. Apart from being illegal, it will seriously effect carburation. The resulting weak mixture and overheating may cause an engine siezure. Running without the baffle will not increase the performance of the machine. The reverse, infact, is the case because of the designed effect of exhaust back-pressure on the engine. This may also apply if a non-standard silencer is fitted.

13 Fault diagnosis: fuel system and lubrication

Symptom	Cause	Remedy
Engine gradually fades and stops	Fuel starvation	Check vent hole in filler cap and clear if blocked. Sediment in filter bowl or blocking float needle. Dismantle and clean.
Engine runs badly, black smoke from exhausts	Carburettor flooding	Dismantle and clean carburettor. Look for punctured float.
Engine lacks response and overheats	Weak mixture Air filter disconnected or hoses split	Check for partial blockage in fuel/carburettor. Reconnect or repair.
White smoke from exhaust	Oil pump setting incorrect, too much oil passing Incorrect oil in oil tank	Check and reset oil pump. Drain and refill with recommended grade.
General lack of response to varying throttle openings	Blocked exhaust system	Remove silencer baffles and clean.

Chapter 3 Ignition system

Contents

Specifications

Spark plug

			A50	A50P	AS50
Make			NGK	NGK	NGK
Type			B - 8 HS	B - 8 HS	B - 77 HC
Size			14 mm	14 mm	14 mm
Contact breaker gap			0.3 - 0.4 mm (0.012 - 0.016 in)	0.3 - 0.4 mm (0.012 - 0.016 in)	0.3 - 0.4 mm (0.012 - 0.016 in)
Ignition timing			$24^\circ \pm 2^\circ$ BTDC (2.03 mm)	$24^\circ \pm 2^\circ$ BTDC (2.03 mm)	$24^\circ \pm 2^\circ$ BTDC (2.03 mm)

1 General description

A conventional contact breaker coil ignition system is used. The contact breaker is operated by a cam on the alternator rotor. The opening and closing of the contact breaker every revolution causes a magnetic field in the primary windings of the ignition coil to build up and then collapse. This induces a high voltage in the secondary windings, which causes a spark to occur across the electrodes of the spark plug.

2 Ignition coil: function

The ignition coil consists of primary and secondary windings mounted on a soft iron core. It operates in conjunction with the contact breaker to convert low tension voltage from the primary coil into high tension voltage necessary for the spark.

3 Ignition coil: location and checking

1 The ignition coil is located under the petrol tank, which has to be removed to give access (See Chapter 2, Section 2).
2 The ignition coil is a sealed unit, designed to give long service without need for attention. If a weak spark, no spark at all or difficult starting causes the performance of the coil to be suspect, it should be tested by a Suzuki agent or auto-electrical specialist who will have the appropriate test equipment. A faulty coil must be renewed since it is not possible to effect a satisfactory repair.
3 A defective condenser can give the illusion of a faulty coil and for this reason it is advisable to investigate the condition of the condenser before condemning the ignition coil.

4 Condenser: function and location

1 The condenser has two functions. Firstly it reduces sparking at the control breaker points (and hence prevents rapid wear of the points). Its second and more important function is to greatly increase the induced voltage in the secondary windings of the coil and hence the strength of the high tension spark at break. In practice, without the condenser the spark is very weak and the machine does not run smoothly.
2 The condenser is located on the stator plate and is held in position by one crosshead screw.

4.2. Condenser is held in position by one screw

3 If the condenser is suspected of malfunctioning, it should be removed and replaced with a new item. There is no easy way of checking the condenser without the appropriate test equipment and it is more convenient to cross-check by substitution, especially in view of the low cost of this component.

4 The usual signs of a defective condenser are a weak 'thin' spark and the blackened and burnt appearance of the faces of the contact breaker points due to arcing. A small amount of arcing is inevitable, but never an intense spark at every opening and closing.

5 Contact breaker: examination, renovation and adjustment

1 To renew the contact breaker assembly or to remove it for cleaning purposes, both the left-hand engine cover (and gear lever) and the alternator rotor have to be removed. If adjustment only is required, removal of the circular inspection cover is sufficient for access.

2 To adjust the contact breaker, remove the two inspection cover screws and cover. The contact breaker gap should be checked at its widest opening, with feeler gauges, through the inspection hole of the rotor.

3 To remove the contact breaker assembly, detach the gear lever and the screws retaining the pedal chain cover in the case of the A50P model. Remove the screws retaining the left-hand engine cover and lift off the cover. Put the machine in gear, apply the rear brake and undo the rotor nut. Remove the nut and rotor, and if necessary, remove the Woodruff key. Remove the retaining screw and circlip (noting any shims which may be fitted) and remove the wire from the coil. Lift off the points assembly.

4 Check the contact breaker points for pitting and burning. If this is only slight it can be removed by the use of an oil stone or needle file. If severe or if the contacts do not meet squarely, renew the contact breaker assembly.

5 When refitting, lightly grease the contact breaker pin with a graphited or molybdenum grease.

6 Soak the lubricating felt pad in hypoid oil and squeeze out the excess before refitting.

7 Reassemble in the reverse order to dismantling. Always check the accuracy of the ignition timing and adjust, if necessary.

6 Ignition timing: checking and adjustment

1 Check the ignition timing after having cleaned and set the contact breaker assembly.

2 Turn the engine by hand in the normal direction of rotation (anticlockwise) until the points just commence to open. At this point the arrow on the rotor's flat outer face should align with

5.2a Check gap at its widest opening

5.2b To adjust the gap, loosen this screw

5.3 To remove, detach screw and prise off the circlip

6.2 Arrow must align with crankcase mark

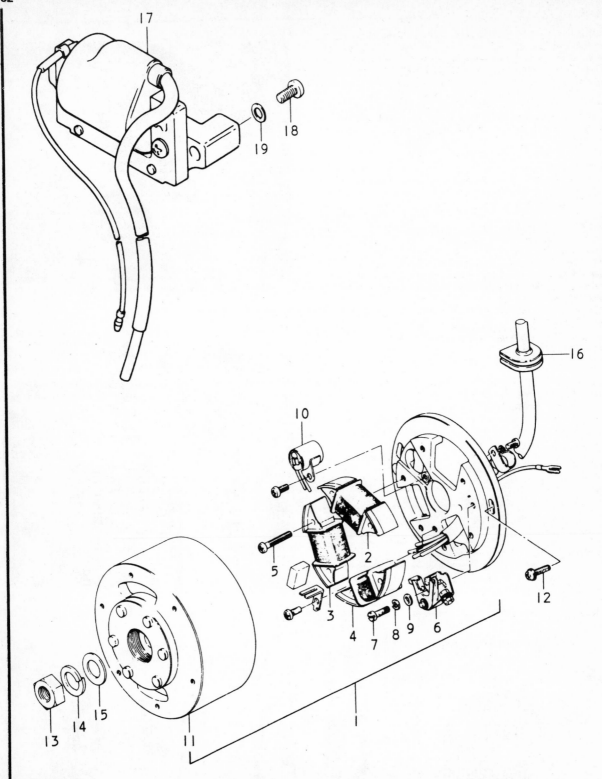

Fig. 3.1. Flywheel magneto and ignition coil

1	Flywheel magneto assembly	5	Screw - 6 off	10	Condenser	15	Washer
2	Lighting coil 1	6	Contact points assembly	11	Flywheel rotor	16	Grommet
3	Lighting coil 2	7	Screw	12	Screw - 3 off	17	Ignition coil assembly
4	Primary ignition coil	8	Lockwasher	13	Nut	18	Screw - 2 off
		9	Washer	14	Lockwasher	19	Washer - 2 off

Fig. 3.2a. Spark plug maintenance

Checking plug gap with feeler gauges

Altering the plug gap. Note use of correct tool

Fig. 3.2b. Spark plug electrode condition

A *White deposits and damaged porcelain insulation indicating overheating*

B *Broken porcelain insulation due to bent central electrode*

C *Electrodes burnt away due to wrong heat valve or chronic pre-ignition (pinking)*

D *Excessive black deposits caused by over-rich mixture or wrong heat valve*

E *Mild white deposits and electrode burnt indicating too weak a fuel mixture*

F *Plug in sound condition with light greyish brown deposits*

A

B

C

D

E

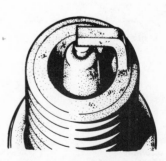

F

the cast pointer in the left-hand engine cover (at approximately 5-o'clock). If this cannot be achieved, proceed to the next operation.

3   Remove the left-hand engine cover and turn the rotor in the normal direction of rotation, by hand, until the points just begin to open. At this point, the mark on the rotor rim should align with the cast pointer in the engine crankcase (at approximately 8 o'clock). As these marks provide only a rough guide and are not sufficiently accurate for timing purposes, a dial gauge must be used to achieve the 2.03 mm before top dead centre (BTDC) at which the points should commence to separate.

4   To alter the timing, the whole stator plate has to be rotated. The plate is held by three screws in elongated slots. Slacken the screws and rotate the plate so that the points just begin to open when the dial gauge reads 2.03 mm BTDC, (with the points gap set at 0.35 mm). The actual opening of the points can be assessed visually with a 0.05 mm (0.0015 in) feeler gauge.

7   Spark plug: checking and resetting the gap

1   The A50 and A50P models are fitted with a NGK B - 8HS spark plug as standard, gapped within the range 0.6 - 0.7 mm (0.024 - 0.028 in). Certain operating conditions may indicate a change in spark plug grade, although the type recommended by the manufacturer will usually give the best, all round service. The AS50 model has an NGK B - 77 HC plug.

2   Check the plug gap during every three monthly or two thousand mile service. To reset the gap, bend the outer electrode until the correct feeler gauge can be inserted. Never try to bend the centre electrode or the insulation will crack and render the plug unserviceable.

3   With some experience, the condition of the spark plug electrode and insulator can be used as a reliable guide to engine operating conditions.

4   Beware of overtightening the spark plug, otherwise there is a risk of stripping the threads in the aluminium alloy head. Use a spanner which is a good fit, to prevent the spanner slipping and breaking the insulation.

5   If the threads in the cylinder head strip as a result of over-tightening the spark plug, it is possible to reclaim the head with the use of Helcoil thread insert. This is a cheap and convenient method of replacing the threads; most motor cycle dealers operate a service of this kind.

6   Make sure the plug insulating cap is a good fit and has its rubber seal. It should also be kept clean to prevent tracking. The cap contains a suppressor that eliminates both radio and television interference.

6.3 These marks must align exactly - stator plate ...

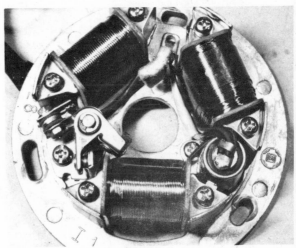

6.4 ... has elongated slots to permit movement

8   Fault diagnosis: ignition system

Symptom	Cause	Remedy
Engine will not start	No spark at plug	Faulty ignition switch. Check whether current is reaching ignition coil.
	Weak spark at plug	Dirty contact breaker points require cleaning. Contact breaker gaps have closed up. Reset.
Engine starts, but runs erratically	Intermittent or weak spark	Renew plug. If no improvement check whether points are arcing. If so, replace condenser.
	Ignition over-advanced	Check ignition timing and if necessary reset .
	Plug lead insulation breaking down	Check for breaks in outer covering, especially near frame and plug cap.
Engine difficult to start and runs sluggishly. Overheats	Ignition timing retarded	Check ignition timing and advance to correct setting.

Chapter 4 Frame and forks

Contents

Specifications

Steering lock	45° (left and right)
Caster	63°
Trail	69 mm (2.8 in)
Turning radius	1.7 m (67 in)
Front fork leg oil capacity (each)	138 cc (0.23 Imp pints)

1 Front forks: removal

1 To remove the front forks complete with front wheel, bottom
yoke and steering stem, follow operations 2 - 5 of this Section.
If, however, it is necessary only to remove the fork legs, refer
to operation 6 of this Section.
2 Remove the front brake cable nut and free the cable.
3 Unscrew the speedometer drive cable nut and free the
cable.

4 Remove the domed steering column bolt and also the two
fork stanchion top bolts. This frees the top yoke of the steering
head stem which can be lifted off, complete with handlebars.
5 Slacken and remove the steering column lock and adjuster
nuts, using a C-spanner. The forks are now free and can be
lowered out of the steering head. Take care not to lose the
ball bearings that will fall out as the bearing cups and cones
separate.
6 Remove the front wheel, as described in Chapter 5, Section 3.
Remove the mudguard by undoing the four securing bolts and

1.6a Remove the bolts securing the mudguard

1.6b Unscrew and remove the stanchion bolts

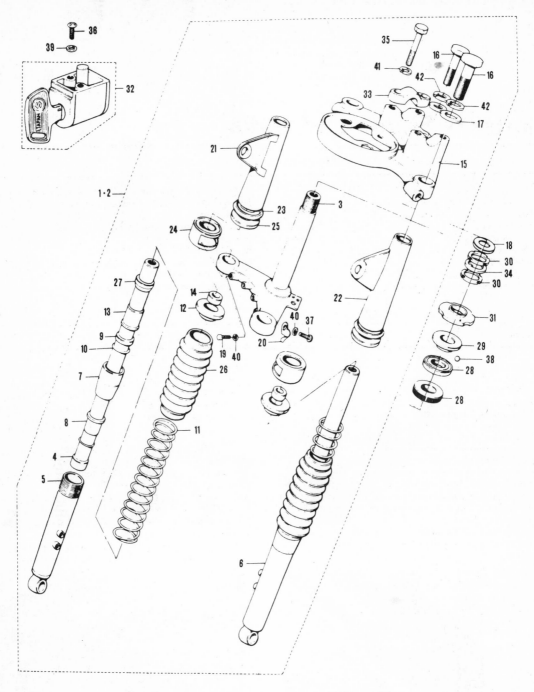

Fig. 4.1a. Front forks - AS50 and A50 models

1 Front forks - complete	12 Spring seat - 2 off	23 Bracket seat - 2 off	33 Handlebar clamp - 2 off
2 Front forks - complete	13 Dust excluder - 2 off	24 Yoke trim - 2 off	34 Steering lockwasher
3 Bottom yoke/steering stem	14 Damper piece - 2 off	25 Rubber cushion - 2off	35 Bolts - 4 off
4 Stanchion - 2 off	15 Upper (crown) yoke	26 Spring gaiter - 2 off	36 Screw - 2 off
5 RH lower fork leg	16 Fork cap bolt - 2 off	27 Spring guide - 2 off	37 Screw
6 LH lower fork leg	17 Plain washer - 3 off	28 Steering head bearing	38 Steel ball - 44 off
7 Slider bush housing - 2 off	18 Cover plate	cup - 2 off	39 Spring washer - 2 off
8 Slider bush - 2 off	19 Pinch bolt - 2 off	29 Steering head bearing cone	40 Spring washer
9 Oil seal - 2 off	20 Brake cable clip	30 Adjuster nut - 2 off	41 Spring washer - 4 off
10 Lower 'O' ring - 2 off	21 RH headlamp bracket	31 Dust seal	42 Spring washer - 5 off
11 Fork spring - 2 off	22 LH headlamp bracket	32 Steering lock	

washers. Slacken the pinch bolt in the lower fork yoke. The fork leg can now be removed downwards. Repeat the procedure for the other fork leg.

2 Front fork legs: dismantling, examination and replacement

1 Invert the fork leg to drain off the oil and remove the upper spring guide, spring and lower spring guide.

2 Holding the lower fork leg in a vice, wrap some rag or rubber strip around the fork leg nut and using a chain wrench loosen, and remove the shroud nut.

3 Separate the lower fork leg and stanchion, note the O-ring in the top of the stanchion.

4 If the fork action was 'sticky' check that the fork stanchion is not bent or distorted. If it is bent a new stanchion will have to be obtained. It is not advisable to try and straighten it without the appropriate equipment.

1.6c Slacken the pinch bolt

2.1 Remove the upper spring guide, spring and lower spring guide

2.2a Unscrew the fork leg nut with a chain wrench

2.2b Loosen and remove the fork leg nut

2.3 Note the 'O' ring in the top of the stanchion

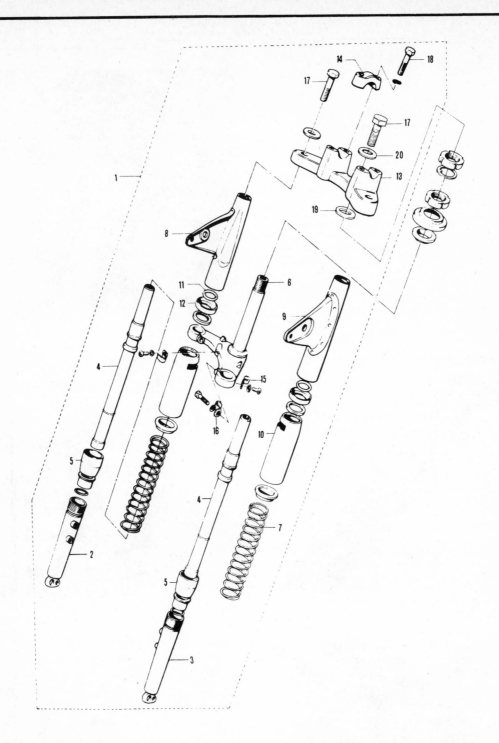

Fig. 4.1b. Front forks - A50 Mk II

1	Front forks complete	11	'O' ring - 2 off
2	RH lower fork leg	12	Bracket seat - 2 off
3	LH lower fork leg	13	Upper (crown) yoke
4	Stanchion - 2 off	14	Handlebar clamp - 2 off
5	Stanchion bush	15	Clip
	housing - 2 off	16	Clip
6	Lower yoke/steering stem	17	Cap bolt - 3 off
7	Fork spring - 2 off	18	Bolt - 4 off
8	RH headlamp bracket	19	Plain washer
9	LH headlamp bracket	20	Plain washer
10	Lower shroud - 2 off		

5   Check the condition of the oil seal in the fork leg nut and fit a new one if in doubt about its condition. An O-ring is also fitted to the shroud below the thread and this also should be . renewed.

6   Thoroughly clean the components and oil them with the correct grade of fork oil. Reassemble in the reverse order of dismantling.

3 Front forks: replacement

1   Front fork replacement is the reversal of the dismantling procedure. It will assist assembly if the long bolt which secures the swinging arm can be used, to pull the stanchion and shroud up and against the spring, whilst at the same time, tightening the clamp bolt. Remove the swinging arm bolt and fit the stanchion top bolt. Loosen the clamp bolt and finally position the fork legs by tightening the top bolt. Retighten the clamp bolt.

2   If the complete forks have been removed, the steering head bearings will need adjustment. See Section 6 of this Chapter.

3   To refill with fork oil, remove each fork stanchion top bolt and using a suitable container, top up the forks. Gently work the forks to settle them. Refit the top bolts.

4 Fork leg oil: changing

1   Some models are fitted with a drain plug in the base of the lower fork leg, others have no facility for draining. On models without a drain plug, drain the fork by removing the complete fork leg (see Section 1.6) from the machine and inverting it to allow the oil to drain out.

2   On models fitted with drain plugs remove the plugs and slacken the fork stanchion bolts; pump the forks to expel all the oil. Replace the drain plugs when all oil is drained off.

3   Remove the fork stanchion bolts and refill each leg with 133 cc (0.23 imp pints) of SAE30 oil. Replace and tighten the two top bolts.

5 Steering head bearings: examination and replacement

1   Before assembly of the forks is commenced, examine the steering head races. The ball bearing tracks of the cup and cone bearings should be polished and free from cracks and

2.5a Oil seal is within the fork nut

2.5b An 'O' ring is fitted to the lower fork leg

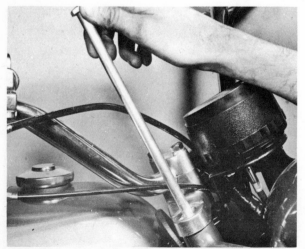
3.1 Swinging arm bolt can be used to pull fork leg into position

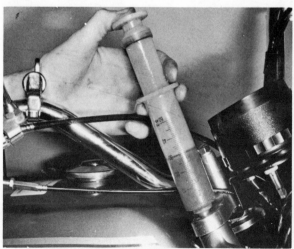
3.3 Refill fork leg with correct amount of fluid

6.2 Use a 'C' spanner to slacken the stem nut

8.1 Bolts thread into swinging arm

9.1 Remove nut and washer from cotter pin

9.3 Slide off cap and dust seal

indentations. If wear or damage is evident, the cups and cones must be renewed as a complete set.

2   Ball bearings are inexpensive, therefore if the originals are marked or discoloured they should be renewed. To assist in holding the steel balls in position, pack the bearings with grease. It will be found that with the correct number of ball bearings in each race (equal number in each) that there is space for the addition of ONE ball. The space must be left free to prevent the balls 'skidding' together and greatly accelerating wear.

6   Steering head: adjustment

1   Slacken the steering stem nut of the steering stem head.
2   Using a C-spanner, slacken the lock ring of the steering stem. Adjustment of the steering head bearings is made by turning the ring nut. Do not overtighten the bearings otherwise the handling characteristics of the machine will be affected. It is possible to overtighten so that the increased load on the bearings will accelerate wear. As a guide, only very slight pressure should be needed to start the forks turning to either side under their own weight, when the front wheel is raised off the ground. Check also that the bearings are not too slack; there should be no discernable movement of the forks in the fore and aft direction.
3   Tighten the lock ring whilst holding the ring nut. Check that the adjustment has not changed; readjust as necessary.
4   Loose steering head bearings will cause the fork to judder when the front brake is applied hard. Overtight bearings will give rise to a characteristic low speed roll, making it difficult to steer in a straight line.

7   Steering lock: location and removal

1   The steering lock is secured by two screws to a bracket on the steering head stem. Removal is by undoing the two screws.
2   Note that if the steering head lock is changed new keys will be required.

8   Rear suspension units: removal, examination and setting

1   Both rear suspension units are held by one long through bolt at the top and separate bolts at the bottom. Note that the bottom bolts are threaded into the swinging arm, so that the

domed nuts must be removed first and then the bolt unscrewed from the swinging arm. Replacement is reversal of removal.

2   The suspension units are sealed and there is no means of topping up or changing the damping fluid. If the unit fails or breaks, renewal is necessary.

9   Pedals and shaft assembly: removal and replacement

1   On the A50P models only, pedals are fitted. To remove the assembly, first remove the nut and washer from the left-hand crank cotter pin, tap out the pin and remove the pedal and crank.

2   Remove the screws securing the pedal chain cover and remove the cover. Disconnect the pedal chain and remove it. Take off the circlip from the cycle crank shaft. The right-hand pedal and positioner can now be extracted from the right-hand side of the machine.

3   Dismantle the assembly by sliding the cap and dust seal along the crank to disclose the positioner assembly. Remove the circlip, pedal crank, outer dog, dust cover, sleeve, spring inner dust cover and inner stopper dog assembly and circlip. Do not forget the Woodruff key.

4   Examine the components for damage and renew as necessary. Assembly is in the reverse of dismantling.

10 Swinging arm rear fork: removal, examination and assembly

1   To detach the swinging arm, remove the rear wheel as described in Chapter 5, Section 5. Also remove the final drive chain at its spring link.

2   Remove both the bottom domed nuts of the suspension units and unscrew the bolts from the swinging arm.

3   Undo the swinging arm pivot bolt nut and withdraw the bolt. The swinging arm can now be lifted out of the frame. Note the plastic chain protector fitted to the left-hand side.

4   Check the condition of the rubber bushes and renew as necessary. Check the pivot for wear and trueness. The old bushes can be pressed out, using the new ones. A vice and a socket of suitable diameter, used as a spacer, can be utilised for this purpose.

5   Place a straight metal bar across the open ends of the swinging arm, where the rear wheel spindle is normally located. Check for twist and misalignment, A twisted swinging arm will throw the wheel out of true and offset the machines handling.

6   To assemble, reverse the dismantling procedure.

7   Do not tighten the swinging arm pivot bolt nut until the arm is in its normal working position. (ie; with the suspension units connected) otherwise the bonded bushes will be placed under a permanent torque loading.

11 Frame: examination and renovation

1   The frame is unlikely to require attention unless accident damage has occurred. In some cases, replacement of the frame is the only satisfactory course of action if it is badly out of alignment. Only a few frame repair specialists have the jigs and mandrels necessary for resetting the frame to the required standard of accuracy and even then there is no easy means of assessing to what extent the frame may have been overstressed.

2   After the machine has covered a considerable mileage, it is advisable to examine the frame closely for signs of cracking or splitting at the welded joint. Rust corrosion can also cause weakness at these joints. Minor damage can be repaired by welding or brazing, depending on the extent and nature of the damage.

3   Remember that a frame which is out of alignment will cause handling problems and may even promote 'speed wobbles'. If misalignment is suspected, as the result of an accident, it will be necessary to strip the machine completely so that the frame can be checked and, if necessary, renewed.

10.3a Withdraw the pivot bolt

10.3b Swinging arm fork can be lifted from frame

10.4 Check condition of rubber bushes

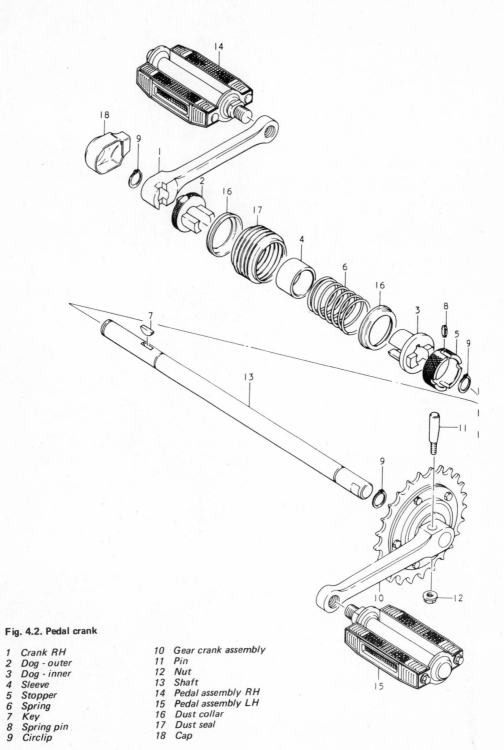

Fig. 4.2. Pedal crank

1	Crank RH	10	Gear crank assembly
2	Dog - outer	11	Pin
3	Dog - inner	12	Nut
4	Sleeve	13	Shaft
5	Stopper	14	Pedal assembly RH
6	Spring	15	Pedal assembly LH
7	Key	16	Dust collar
8	Spring pin	17	Dust seal
9	Circlip	18	Cap

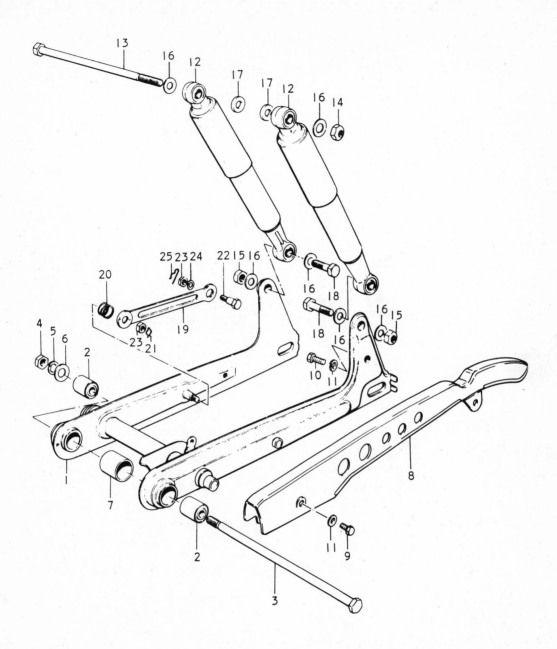

Fig. 4.3. Rear swinging arm

1 Swinging arm assembly	7 Cushion	13 Shaft	19 Torque link
2 Bush	8 Chain case	14 Nut	20 Spring
3 Shaft	9 Bolt	15 Nut	21 Clip
4 Nut	10 Bolt	16 Washer	22 Bolt
5 Lockwasher	11 Washer	17 Washer	23 Nut
6 Washer	12 Shock absorber	18 Bolt	24 Lockwasher
			25 Clip

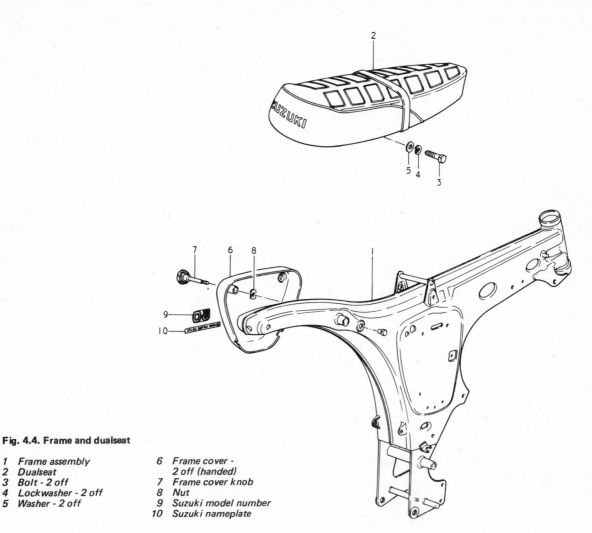

Fig. 4.4. Frame and dualseat

1 *Frame assembly*	6 *Frame cover -*
2 *Dualseat*	*2 off (handed)*
3 *Bolt - 2 off*	7 *Frame cover knob*
4 *Lockwasher - 2 off*	8 *Nut*
5 *Washer - 2 off*	9 *Suzuki model number*
	10 *Suzuki nameplate*

12 Footrests: renovation

1   If the footrests have become bent, as may occur if the machine has been dropped, they can be straightened by heating and bending.
2   Remove the footrest bar from the machine by undoing the two front bolts and slackening the two at the rear. Remove the footrest rubbers.
3   Heat the footrest bar, playing a blowlamp on the bent section whilst holding it in a vice and then bend it back to its original shape. Never attempt to straighten the bar whilst it is still attached to the machine, since this will place a severe strain on the mounting points.
4   To renew the rear footrest rubbers, remove the split pin and pull out the clevis pin. The old rubber can now be slid off.

13 Centre and prop stand: examination

1   The centre stand is attached to the lower part of the frame and provides a convenient means of parking the machine. A prop stand is also fitted to some machines, which provides a means for very quick parking and for use on sloping ground.
2   Both stands have return springs and the return action of each stand should be checked regularly. If either stand falls whilst the machine is in motion, it could catch in the ground and cause an accident. If in doubt, renew the springs. Make sure the pivot bolts are tight, unworn and well lubricated.

14 Speedometer cable: examination and renovation

1   It is advisable to detach the speedometer drive cable from time to time in order to check whether it is adequately lubricated and whether the outer covering is compressed or damaged at any point along its run. A jerky or sluggish speedometer operation can often be attributed to a cable fault.
2   To grease the cable, withdraw the inner cable. After removing the old grease, clean with a petrol soaked rag and examine the cable for broken strands or other damage.
3   Grease the cable with high melting point grease, taking care

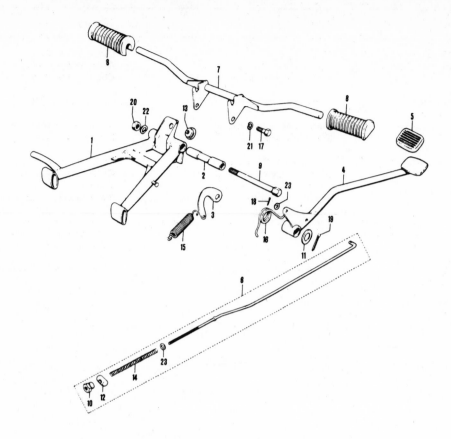

Fig. 4.5. Front footrests and centre stand

1	Centre stand	12	Trunnion
2	Centre stand bush	13	Buffer
3	Spring plate	14	Spring
4	Rear brake pedal	15	Stand return spring
5	Pedal rubber	16	Pedal return spring
6	Brake rod assembly	17	Bolt - 2 off
7	Footrest bar	18	Split pin
8	Footrest rubber - 2 off	19	Split pin
9	Bolt	20	Nut
10	Brake adjuster nut	21	Spring washer - 2 off
11	Plain washer	22	Spring washer
		23	Plain washer

not to grease the last six inches at the point where the cable enters the speedometer head. If this precaution is not observed, grease will work its way into the speedometer head and immobilise it.

4   If both the speedometer head and mileage recorder stop working, it is probable that the cable has broken. If so, the inner cable alone can be renewed and reinserted in the outer casing after greasing. Never fit a new inner cable alone if the outer casing is damaged or compressed at any point along its run.

15 Cleaning the machine

1   After removing all surface dirt with a rag or sponge which is washed frequently in clean water, the machine should be allowed to dry thoroughly. Application of car polish or wax to the cycle parts will give a good finish, particularly if the machine receives this attention at regualr intervals.

2   The plated parts should require only a wipe with a damp rag, but if they are badly corroded, as may occur during the

winter when the roads are salted, it is permissible to use one of the proprietary chrome cleaners. These often have an oil base which will help to prevent corrosion from recurring.

3   If the engine parts are particularly oily, use a cleaning compound such as 'Gunk' or 'Jizer'. Apply the compound whilst the parts are dry and work it in with a brush so that it has an opportunity to penetrate and soak into the film of oil and grease. Finish off by washing down liberally, taking care that water does not enter the carburettor, air cleaner or the electrics. If desired, the now clean aluminium alloy parts can be enhanced still further when they are dry by using a special polish such as Solvol Autosol. This will restore the full lustre.

4   If possible, the machine should be wiped down immediately after it has been used in the wet, so that it is not garaged under damp conditions that will promote rusting. Make sure the chain is wiped and re-oiled, to prevent water from entering the rollers and causing harshness with an accompanying rapid rate of wear. Remember that there is less chance of water entering the control cables and causing stiffness if they are lubricated regularly as described in The Routine Maintenance Section.

16 Fault diagnosis: frame and forks

Symptom	Cause	Remedy
Machine veers either to the left or the right with hands off handlebars	Bent frame Twisted forks· Wheels out of alignment	Check and renew. Check and renew. Check and re-align.
Machine rolls at low speed	Overtight steering head bearings	Slacken until adjustment is correct.
Machine judders when front brake is applied	Slack steering head bearings Worn fork legs	Tighten until adjustment is correct. Renew worn parts.
Machine pitches on uneven surfaces	Ineffective fork dampers Ineffective rear suspension units Suspension too soft	Check oil content. Check whether units still have damping action. Raise suspension unit adjustment one notch.
Fork action stiff	Fork legs out of alignment (twisted in yokes)	Slacken yoke clamps, and fork top bolts. Pump fork several times then retighten from bottom upwards.
Machine wanders. Steering imprecise. Rear wheel tends to hop	Worn swinging arm pivot	Dismantle and renew bushes and pivot shaft.

Chapter 5 Wheels, brakes and tyres

Contents

Specifications

Brakes
Front and rear ... ...   Drum type, single leading shoe

Tyre size (in)
Front and rear ... ...   2.25 - 17 - 4PR

---

1 General description

Both wheels fitted to the A50, A50P and AS50 models are of the same diameter and width. The front wheel is fitted with a ribbed tyre and a block tread tyre is fitted to the rear as standard. The single leading shoe brakes are of the same diameter and width and utilise identical shoes. The wheels are not interchangeable

2 Wheels: examination and renovation

1   Place the machine firmly on blocks so that the wheel is raised clear of the ground. Spin the wheel and by using a pointer, such as a screwdriver, check the wheel rim alignment.
    Small irregularities can be corrected by tightening the spokes in the affected area, although a certain amount of experience is advisable to prevent over-correction. Any flats in the wheel rim should be evident at the same time. These are more difficult to

remove and in most cases it will be necessary to have the wheel rebuilt on a new rim. Apart from the effect on stability a flat will expose the tyre bead and walls to greater risk or damage if the machine is run with a deformed wheel.

2   Check for loose and broken spokes. Tapping the spokes is a good guide to tension. A loose spoke will produce a quite different sound and should be tightened by turning the nipple in an anticlockwise direction. Always recheck for run-out by spinning the wheel again. If the spokes have to be tightened an excessive amount, it is advisable to remove both tyre and tube by following the procedure in Section 13 of this Chapter. This is so that the protruding ends of the spokes can be ground off, to prevent them chafing the inner tube and causing punctures.

---

3 Front wheel: removal and replacement

1   Place the machine on its centre stand. Disconnect the brake cable at the brake operating lever and unscrew the speedometer drive cable.

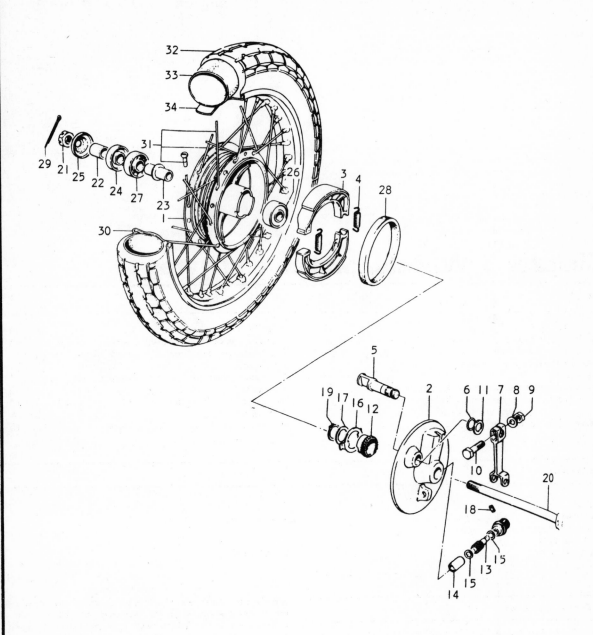

Fig. 5.1. Front wheel

1	Drum	9	Nut	17	Thrust washer	26	Bearing LH
2	Backplate	10	Bolt	18	Screw	27	Bearing RH
3	Shoe	11	Washer	19	Circlip	28	Oil seal
4	Spring	12	Gear - speedometer	20	Scale	29	Split pin
5	Camshaft	13	Pinion	21	Nut	30	Wheel rim
6	Dust seal	14	Bush	22	Spacer, axle LH	31	Spoke set
7	Lever	15	Thrust washer	23	Spacer, hub bearing	32	Tyre
8	Washer	16	Driver	24	Oil seal	33	Tube
				25	Cover	34	Protector

2   Remove the split pin and wheel spindle nut and withdraw the wheel spindle.

3   Lift the wheel and brake assembly from the machine. Note the spacer and dust cover fitted on the right-hand side of the hub.

4   To replace the wheel reverse the above procedure. Make sure the brake plate recess locates over the lug on the lower fork leg. Before finally tightening the spindle nut, operate the forks, spin the wheel and operate the brake. Firstly, this aligns the fork leg and secondly it centralises the brake shoes in the drum. Make doubly certain the brake plate recess is correctly located over the lug on the lower fork leg to prevent the plate from turning when braking. Fit a new split pin in the wheel spindle nut.

4   Speedometer drive gearbox: examination and maintenance

1   The speedometer drive gearbox is incorporated in the brake plate of the front wheel and should give little trouble. Drive from the wheel is via a special driver washer. To obtain access first remove the front wheel as described in preceding Section and take out the brake plate assembly complete.

2   To dismantle the drive pinion assembly remove the circlips,

3.1a Disconnect the brake cable and ...

3.1b ... unscrew the speedometer cable

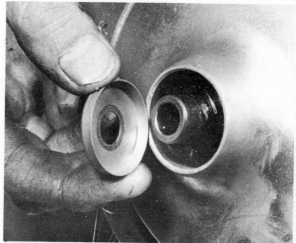

3.3 Note the spacer and dust cover

3.4 Brake plate locates over fork lug

4.2 Remove the circlip

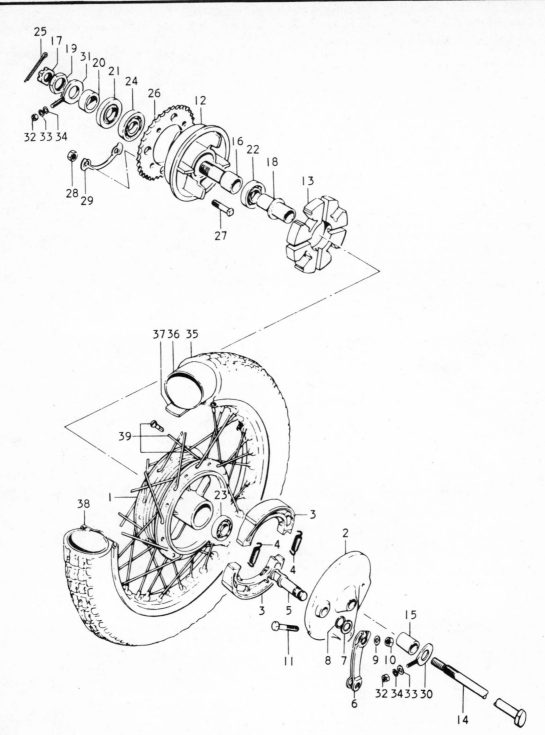

Fig. 5.2. Rear wheel

1 Drum	11 Bolt	21 Oil seal	31 Adjuster LH
2 Backplate	12 Drum - sprocket	22 Bearing, LH	32 Nut
3 Shoe	13 Shock absorber	23 Bearing, RH	33 Washer
4 Spring	14 Rear wheel spindle	24 Bearing, sprocket drum	34 Lockwasher
5 Camshaft	15 Spindle spacer	25 Split pin	35 Tyre
6 Lever	16 Sprocket spindle	26 Sprocket	36 Tube
7 Washer	17 Nut	27 Bolt	37 Rim band
8 Dust seal	18 Spacer	28 Nut	38 Rim
9 Washer	19 Nut	29 Washer	39 Spoke set
10 Nut	20 Spacer	30 Adjuster RH	

thrust washer, driver washer, drive pinion and thrust washer. The worm gear is retained in the brake plate by a grub screw. Again, two thrust washers are fitted.

3 Assemble in the reverse order of dismantling. Lightly lubricate the gears with high melting point grease. Ensure that the large oil seal is in good condition; renew it if in doubt, since if it is damaged, grease will work through and contaminate the brake linings.

5 Rear wheel and brake: removal and replacement

1 All three models are fitted with a quickly detachable rear wheel which makes it unnecessary to remove the final drive chain.

2 Place the machine on its centre stand. Undo the brake rod adjuster nut, depress the brake pedal and remove the rod from the brake lever trunnion. Do not mislay the trunnion and spring.

3 Remove the 'R' clip and nut on the brake end of the torque arm and free the arm from the backplate.

4 Remove the split pin and undo the rear wheel outer spindle nut. Withdraw the wheel spindle complete with chain adjuster. Note the spacer fitted on the right-hand side. Lift out the brake plate and shoes.

5 Pull the wheel over to the right-hand side to free the cush drive and lift the wheel clear by tilting the machine to the left to obtain clearance.

6 Replacement is by reversing the removal procedure. Do not forget the spacer or the right-hand side over the 'R' clip on the torque arm nut. The rear brake will need to be adjusted. Before tightening the wheel spindle nut, spin the wheel and apply the brake to centralise the brake shoes in the drum. Use a new split pin after tightening the spindle nut.

6 Brakes: dismantling, examination and replacement

1 Both front and rear brakes are of the single leading shoe type and for servicing purposes can be treated alike.

2 Remove the wheel and brake as described in Section 3 for the front wheel or Section 5 for the rear wheel. Note that in the case of the rear brake it is not necessary to remove the rear wheel completely, only to proceed as far as withdrawing the wheel spindle and removing the spacer. This then provides sufficient clearance to remove the brake plate and brake shoes.

3 Examine the condition of the brake linings. If they are

5.3 Remove the 'R' clip and nut

5.4 Spindle will withdraw complete with chain adjuster

5.5 Wheel will pull off sprocket to expose cush drive

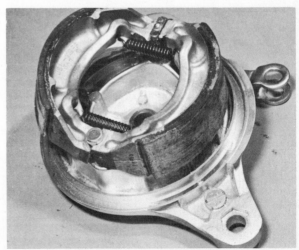
6.3 Examine the condition of the brake linings

6.5 Check operation of brake cam before replacing brake shoes

7.1 Wheel bearings have integral oil seals

wearing thin or unevenly the brake shoes should be renewed. The linings are bonded to the brake shoes and cannot be supplied separately.

4   To remove the brake shoes, pull them away from the cam and pivot, and then pull them away from the brake plate in a 'V' formation so that they can be lifted away together with the return springs. When they are well clear of the brake plate, the return springs can be disconnected.

5   Before replacing the brake shoes, check that the operating cam is working smoothly and not binding in its housing. The cam can be removed for greasing by detaching the operating arm from the end of the shaft. The operating arm is located on the cam shaft by splines, and is retained by a pinch bolt, mark both the operating arm and the shaft end before removal to aid correct relocation.

6   Check the inner surface of the brake drum, on which the brake shoes bear. The surface should be free from indentations and score marks, otherwise reduced braking efficiency and accelerated brake lining wear will result. Remove all traces of brake lining dust and wipe the drum surface with a petrol soaked rag, to remove all traces of grease and oil.

7   To reassemble the brake shoes on the brake plate, fit the return springs and pull the shoes apart whilst holding them in the form of a 'V' facing upwards. If they are now located with the brake operating cam and fixed pivot, they can be pushed into position by pressing downwards. Do not use excessive force, or there is risk of distorting the shoes. Note: A wear limit is stamped on both drums and an indicator mark is cast on the brake plate.

7   Wheel bearings: removal and replacement

1   The ball journal wheel bearings are all fitted with integral oil seals, although an extra seal is located on the right-hand side of the front wheel.

2   The bearings are a drive fit in the hub and are removed by driving them out with a drift, working from each side of the hub. When the first bearing emerges from the hub, the hollow distance collar that separates the bearing can be removed.

3   Remove all the grease from the hub and bearings. Check the bearings for play or roughness when they are rotated. If there is any doubt about their condition renew them.

4   Before replacing the bearings, first pack the hub with a new high melting point grease, leave sufficient room for expansion of the grease when it becomes hot. Drift the bearings into the hub using a tubular drift, contacting on only the outer ring of

7.2a Remove bearings by driving them out

7.2b Hollow distance collar separates bearings

the bearing (an appropriate size socket will suffice). When the bearing has only one integral oil seal, make sure this is on the outside. Do not forget the distance collar between the bearings.

5 On the rear wheel a third bearing and an additional oil seal is contained in the sprocket carrier. Drift out the stub spindle and remove the spacer. Prise out the oil seal. The bearing can now be drifted out from the other side of the carrier. Check the bearing as before and again repack with high melting point grease. Refit as for the other wheel bearings. Replace the oil seal (renew if necessary), spacer and spindle.

8 Adjusting the front brake

1 When correctly adjusted there should be not less than 20 - 30 mm (0.8 - 1.2 in) between the end of the brake lever and the twist grip when the brake is applied fully. Turn the adjuster clockwise to increase the distance and anti-clockwise to decrease the distance.

2 Check that the brake pulls off correctly when the handlebar lever is released. Sluggish action is usually indicative of a poorly lubricated control cable, broken or stretched return springs or a tendancy for the brake operating arm to bind in its bush. Rubbing brakes affect performance and can cause severe over heating of the lining, drums and wheel bearings.

9 Adjusting the rear brake

1 If the adjustment of the rear brake is correct, the brake pedal will have to travel up from 20 - 30 mm (0.8 - 1.2 inches). Before the amount of travel is adjusted, the brake pedal position should be set so that the pedal is in the best position for quick operation.

2 The length of travel is controlled by the adjuster at the end of the brake operating arm. If the nut is screwed inwards, travel is decreased and vice versa.

3 Note that it may be necessary to readjust the height of the stop lamp switch if the pedal height has been altered to any marked extent. Refer to Chapter 6, for further details.

10 Cush drive assembly: examination and replacement

1 The cush drive assembly is contained within the left-hand

7.5a Drift out the stub spindle and ...

7.5b ... remove the spacer

7.5c Prise out the oil seal

7.5d Sprocket bearing can now be drifted out

10.1 The cush drive assembly

Fig. 5.3. Checking wheel alignment

A & C   Incorrect
B   Correct

11.2 Remove the nut securing the left-hand adjuster

side of the rear wheel hub. It comprises a synthetic rubber buffer housed within a series of vanes cast in the hub shell. A plate attached to the rear wheel sprocket has six cast-in dogs that engage with slots in these rubbers. The drive to the rear wheel is transmitted through these rubbers, which cushion any surges and roughness in the drive which would otherwise convey the impression of harshness.

2   Under normal riding conditions the cush drive rubbers will continue to be serviceable for an extended length of service. The rubbers should be tested in situ by firmly holding the rear wheel and turning the sprocket alternately in a clockwise and anti-clockwise direction. If it is evident that the rubbers have become permanently compressed they should be renewed.

3   The cush drive is a push fit in the rear wheel hub and thus presents no problems to replace.

11 Rear wheel sprocket: removal, examination and replacement

1   The rear wheel sprocket can be detached as a separate unit, after the rear wheel has been removed from the frame, as described in Section 5 of this Chapter, and after the removal of the rear drive chain, as described in the Routine Maintenance Section.

2   Remove the nut securing the left-hand rear wheel adjuster, freeing the rear sprocket assembly. The sprocket is retained to the cush drive plate by four nuts and two lockwashers. The tabs on the lockwashers must be knocked down before loosening the nuts.

3   Check the condition of the sprocket teeth. If they are hooked. chipped or badly worn, the sprocket must be renewed. It is considered bad practice to renew one sprocket on its own. The final drive sprockets should always be renewed as a pair and a new chain fitted, other wise rapid wear will necessitate even earlier renewal on the next occasion.

4   For bearing replacement, refer to Section 7 of this Chapter.

12 Final drive chain: examination, adjustment and lubrication

1   The final drive chain is exposed and periodically the tension will need to be readjusted, to compensate for wear. This is accomplished by slackening the rear wheel nuts after the machine has been placed on the centre stand and drawing the wheel backwards by means of the drawbolt adjusters in the fork ends. The torque arm bolt on the rear brake plate must also be slackened during this operation.

2   The chain is in correct tension if there is from 15 - 20 mm (0.6 - 0.8 in) of slack. Always check when the chain is at its tightest point; a chain rarely wears evenly during service.

3   Always adjust the drawbolts an equal amount in order to preserve wheel alignment. The fork ends are marked with a series of horizontal lines above the adjusters, to provide a visual check. If desired, wheel alignment can be checked by running a plank of wood parallel to the machine, so that it touches both walls of the rear tyre. If wheel alignment is correct, it should be equidistant from either side of the front wheel tyre, when tested on both sides of the rear wheel. It will not touch the front wheel tyre because this tyre is of smaller cross section. See accompanying diagram.

4   Do not run the chain overtight to compensate for uneven wear. A tight chain will place excessive stresses on the gearbox and rear wheel bearings, leading to their early failure. It will also absorb a surprising amount of power.

5   After a period of running, the chain will require lubrication. Lack of oil will accelerate wear of both chain and sprockets and lead to harsh transmission. The application of engine oil will act as a temporary expedient, but it is preferable to remove the chain and immerse it in a molten lubricant such as 'Linklyfe' or 'Chainguard', after it has been cleaned in a paraffin bath. These latter lubricants achieve better penetration of the chain links and rollers and are less likely to be thrown off when the chain is in motion.

6   To check whether the chain requires replacement, lay it
lengthwise in a straight line and compress it endwise until all the
play is taken up. Anchor one end and pull on the other in order
to take up the end play in the opposite direction. If the chain
extends by more than the distance between two adjacent rollers,
it should be replaced in conjunction with the sprockets. Note
that this check should be made after the chain has been washed
out, but before any lubricant is applied, otherwise the lubricant
will take up some of the play.

7   When replacing the chain, make sure the spring link is seated
correctly, with the closed end facing the direction of travel.

8   The chain fitted is of Japanese manufacture. When renewal is
necessary, it should be noted a Renold equivalent, of British
manufacture, is available as an alternative. When obtaining a
replacement, take along the old chain as a pattern and, if known,
a note of the size and number of pitches.

13 Tyres: removal and replacement

1   At some time or other the need will arise to remove and
replace the tyres, either as the result of a puncture or because
replacements are necessary to offset wear. To the inexperienced,
tyre changing represents a formidable task yet if a few simple
rules are observed and the technique learned, the whole operation
is surprisingly simple.

2   To remove the tyre from either wheel, first detach the wheel
from the machine by following the procedure in Section 3 or 5
of this Chapter, depending on whether the front or the rear wheel
is involved. Deflate the tyre by removing the valve insert and when
it is fully deflated, push the bead from the tyre away from the
wheel rim on both sides so that the bead enters the centre well of
the rim. Remove the locking cap and push the tyre valve into the
tyre itself.

3   Insert a tyre lever close to the valve and lever the edges of the
tyre over the outside of the wheel rim. Very little force should
be necessary; if resistance is encountered it is probably due to
the fact that the tyre beads have not entered the well of the
wheel rim all the way round the tyre.

4   Once the tyre has been edged over the wheel rim, it is easy to
work around the wheel rim so that the tyre is completely free on
one side. At this stage, the inner tube can be removed.

5   Working from the other side of the wheel, ease the other
edge of the tyre over the outside of the wheel rim which is
furthest away. Continue to work around the rim until the tyre is
free completely from the rim.

6   If a puncture has necessitated the removal of the tyre, re-
inflate the inner tube and immerse it in a bowl of water to trace
the source of the leak. Mark its position and deflate the tube.
Dry the tube and clean the area around the puncture with a petrol
soaked rag. When the surface has dried, apply rubber solution
and allow this to dry before removing the backing from the patch
and applying the patch to the surface.

7   It is best to use a patch of the self-vulcanising type, which
will form a very permanent repair. Note that it may be necessary
to remove a protective covering from the top surface of the patch,
after it has sealed in position. Inner tubes made from synthetic
rubber may require a special type of patch and adhesive, if a
satisfactory bond it to be achieved.

8   Before replacing tyre, check the inside to make sure the
agent which caused the puncture is not trapped. Check the
outside of the tyre, particularly the tread area to make sure
nothing is trapped which may cause a further puncture.

9   If the inner tube has been patched on a number of past
occasions, or if there is a tear or large hole, it is preferable to
discard it and fit a replacement. Sudden deflation may cause an
accident, particularly if it occurs with the front wheel.

10 To replace the tyre, inflate the inner tube sufficiently for it
to assume a circular shape but only just. Then push it into the
tyre so that it is enclosed completely. Lay the tyre on the wheel
at an angle and insert the valve through the rim tape and the hole
in the wheel rim. Attach the locking cap on the first few threads,

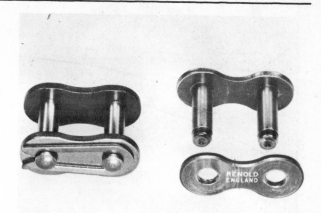

12.3 Renold chain is available as a British replacement

12.7 Closed end must face direction of rotation.

sufficient to hold the valve captive in its correct location.

11 Starting at the point furthest from the valve, push the tyre
bead over the edge of the wheel rim until it is located in the
central well. Continue to work around the tyre in this fashion
until the whole of one side of the tyre is on the rim. It may be
necessary to use a tyre lever during the final stages.

12 Make sure there is no pull on the tyre valve and again
commencing with the area furthest from the valve, ease the other
bead of the tyre over the edge of the rim. Finish with the area
close to the valve, pushing the valve up into the tyre until the
locking cap touches the rim. This will ensure the inner tube is
not trapped when the last section of the bead is edged over the
rim with a tyre lever.

13 Check that the inner tube is not trapped at any point. Re-
inflate the inner tube and check that the tyre is seating correctly
around the wheel rim. There should be a thin rib moulded
around the wall of the tyre on both side, which should be
equidistant from the wheel rim at all points. If the tyre is
unevenly located on the rim, try bouncing the wheel when the
tyre is at the recommended pressure. It is probable that one of
the beads has not pulled clear of the centre well.

14 Always run the tyres at the recommended pressures and never
under or over-inflate. The correct pressures for solo use are
given in the Specifications Section of this Chapter. If a pillion
passenger is carried, increase the rear tyre pressure as recommended.

Fig. 5.4a Tyre removal

A Deflate inner tube and insert lever in close proximity to tyre valve
B Use two levers to work bead over the edge of rim
C When first bead is clear, remove tyre as shown

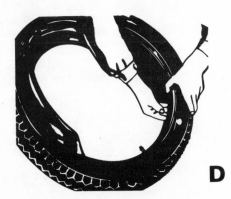

Fig. 5.4b. Tyre replacement

D Inflate inner tube and insert in tyre
E Lay tyre on rim and feed valve through hole in rim
F Work first bead over rim, using lever in final section
G Use similer technique for second bead. Finish at tyre valve position
H Push valve and tube up into tyre when fitting final section, to avoid trapping

15 Tyre replacement is aided by dusting the side walls, particualrly in the vicinity of the beads, with a liberal coating of French chalk. Washing-up liquid can also be used to good effect, but this has the disadvantage of causing the inner surfaces of the wheel rim to rust.

16 Never replace the inner tube and tyre without the rim tape in position. If this precaution is overlooked there is a good chance of the spoke nipples chafing the inner tube causing punctures.

17 Never fit a tyre which has a damaged tread or side walls. Apart from the legal aspects, there is a very great risk of blow-out, which can have serious consequences on any two wheel vehicle.

18 Tyre valves rarely give trouble, but it is always advisable to check whether the valve itself is leaking before removing the tyre. Do not forget to fit the dust cap which forms an effective second seal.

14 Tyre valve dust caps

1 Tyre valve dust caps are often left off when a tyre has been replaced, despite the fact that they serve an important two-fold function. Firstly, they prevent dirt or other foreign matter from entering the valve and causing the valve to stick open when the tyre pump is next applied. Secondly, they form an effective second seal so that in the event of the tyre valve leaking, air will not be lost.

15 Fault diagnosis: wheels, brakes and tyres

Symptom	Cause	Remedy
Handlebars oscillate at low speeds	Buckled front wheel Incorrectly fitted front tyre	Remove wheel for specialist attention. Check whether line around bead is equidistant from rim.
Forks 'hammer' at high speeds	Front wheel out of balance	Add weights until wheel will stop in any position.
Brakes grab, locking wheel	Ends of brake shoes not chamfered	Remove brake shoes and chamfer ends.
Brakes feel spongy	Stretched brake operating cables, weak pull-off springs	Replace cables and/or springs, after inspection.
Tyres wear more rapidily in middle of tread	Over-inflation	Check pressures and run at recommended settings.
Tyres wear rapidly at outer edge of tread	Under-inflation	Ditto.

Chapter 6 Electrical system

Contents

Specifications

Generator	Flywheel alternator
Battery	6V 4 amp hr
Fuse	15 amp
Headlamp	25/25W
Rear/stop light	3/21W
Neutral indicator light	3W
Speedometer light	3W
Direction indicators	8W

All bulbs rated at 6 volts

1 General description

1 All models utilise a twin coil alternator; one coil is in permanent use and the other is switched into circuit when the lights are turned on, thereby supplying the extra current needed.

2 The AC output from the alternator is rectified by a silicon diode (half wave) to provide the DC current for charging the battery. No separate voltage regulator is used.

3 The electrical system is protected by a fuse in the battery positive line. A negative earth is used for the electrical system.

2 Silicon rectifier: function and testing

1 The function of a rectifier is to convert the AC output from the alternator to DC in order to charge the battery. This it does by offering a very low resistance to current flow in one direction

and an extremely high resistance in the reverse. As the ratios of these resistance are very high, one can generalise by saying that an effective current will flow only in one direction.

2 The rectifier is located on the left-hand side of the pressed steel frame, behind the side panel and battery. If it is faulty no repair is possible and a new unit will have to be obtained.

3 The rectifier should not give trouble during normal service. However, it can be damaged by running the machine without a battery, due to the high voltage that is developed by the alternator, or by inadvertently reversing the polarity of the battery.

4 The rectifier can be partially checked by connecting it up in the test circuit shown in the accompanying diagram. Even if the rectifier is shown to be functioning correctly by this test, it does not mean that it is definitely in full working order, since it could still be breaking down under the higher voltages imposed by the alternator. The test does, however, confirm whether the rectifier is faulty due to being in either open or closed circuit.

3 Fuse: location and replacement

1 A 15 amp fuse in a plastic case is located in the battery positive lead and is clipped under the battery retainer. The fuse gives protection from sudden overload, ie; a short circuit.
2 If a fuse blows, the electrical circuit should be checked for a fault before replacing it with another.
3 Always carry at least one spare fuse. This will get you home in an emergency, provided the reason for the original failure has been traced and remedied. Never use a fuse of a higher rating or its protective function will be lost.
4 When a fuse blows whilst the machine is running and no spare fuse is available, a get you home remedy is to remove the blown fuse and to wrap it in silver paper. This will restore electrical continuity by bridging the broken wire within the fuse. This expedient should never be used if there is evidence of a short circuit or other major electrical fault, otherwise more serious damage will be caused. Replace the temporary fuse at the earliest possible opportunity, to restore full circuit protection.

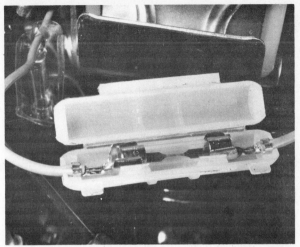

3.1 15 amp fuse is in plastic case

4 Battery: examination and maintenance

1 The electrolyte level of the battery should be maintained between the upper and lower limits marked on the case by topping up with distilled water (unless spillage has occurred when it should be topped up with acid of the correct specific gravity). If, when the battery is in a fully charged condition, (corresponding to approximately 6.6 volts) the specific gravity lies much below 1.26 - 1.28 at 20°C, the electrolyte should be replaced by fresh sulphuric acid of the correct specific gravity (1.26 - 1.28 at 20°C).
2 If the machine will not be used for a while, to prevent deterioration, the battery should be recharged every six weeks or so. If the battery is left in a discharged condition for any length of time the plates will sulphate and render it inoperative.
3 A normal charging rate of 0.4 amp should be used when charging the battery off the machine.
4 If the battery case is cracked or leaking, a replacement battery should be obtained, since it is not often that an effective repair can be made. A leaking battery should never be used, since the acid will severely corrode the cycle parts. If any acid is spilt over the machine or rider, it should be washed off immediately with plenty of water.

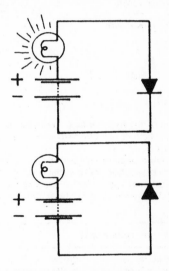

Fig. 6.1. Checking the rectifier

5 Ignition and light switch

1 The ignition and lighting switch are integral and operated by a key which cannot be removed when the ignition is switched on.
2 A replacement key can be obtained if the number on it is quoted.
3 It is not practical to repair the ignition switch if it malfunctions. A new lock and matching key will have to be obtained.

6 Handlebar switches

1 If the switch malfunctions, very little can be done except by cleaning the contacts. If this is ineffective, a replacement unit will have to be obtained.
2 It is worth noting that there are several aerosol-type sprays on the market that are exceptionally good at cleaning switch contacts. Often, this will save needless dismantling, once access has been gained to the contacts themselves.

7 Stop light switch: adjustment

1 The stop light switch is located below the oil tank and is operated by the brake pedal via a spring.

7.1 Stop lamp switch is below the oil tank

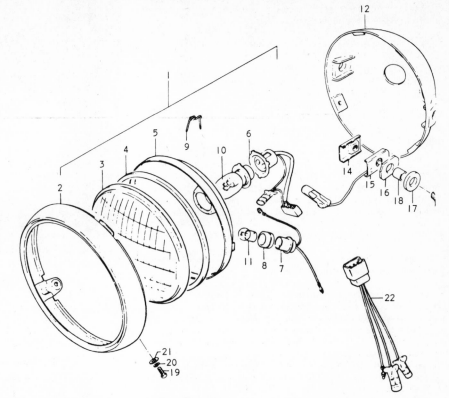

Fig. 6.2. Headlamp

1   Headlamp assembly
2   Rim
3   Lens
4   Sealing gasket
5   Reflector
6   Bulb holder
7   Bulb holder
8   Rubber seal
9   Spring - 3 off
10 Main bulb
11 Pilot bulb
12 Headlamp shell
13 Bolt - 2 off
14 Mounting plate - right hand
15 Mounting plate - left hand
16 Damping rubber 1 - 2 off
17 Damping rubber 2 - 2 off
18 Spacer - 2 off
19 Screw - 2 off
20 Lockwaser - 2 off
21 Washer - 2 off
22 Headlamp lead wire

2   The operation of the switch should always be checked after
adjusting the rear chain or rear brake since these adjustments
may alter the setting.
3   The switch should be actuated when the brake pedal is
depressed and the brake shoes make initial contact with the
brake drum. Adjustment is achieved by screwing the two nuts
down to operate the switch sooner or up to operate it later.

8   Horn: location and replacement

1   The horn is secured by one bolt through its flexible steel
bracket. The bracket is used to isolate the horn from high
frequency vibration. The horn is located under the front of the
petrol tank.
2   It is not practical to adjust the horn and if it malfunctions it
must be renewed (first check its associated wiring and in
particular the horn button earthing). It is a statutory requirement
in most countries that the machine be fitted with a horn in
working order.

9   Indicator flasher: location and replacement

1   If the flasher unit malfunctions it will have to renewed
since repair is impractical.
2   The unit is located under the left-hand side cover and it is
retained in a clip, secured by a screw.
3   If the unit is thought to be malfunctioning, before obtaining
a replacement, check that the flasher bulbs are earthing properly
and that the correct voltage/wattage bulbs have been fitted.

10 Direction indicators: bulb and lens replacement

1   To remove the lens undo the two screws; note the rubber
sealing washer behind the lens.
2   The bulb is of the bayonet type and when renewing, ensure
that the correct wattage (8W) is fitted, otherwise the indicators

will malfunction.
3   When replacing the lens make sure to fit the rubber gasket.
Do not overtighten the screws, or the plastic lens will crack.

11 Headlamp: replacing bulbs and beam height adjustment

1   The headlamp rim is retained by a clip at the top and a screw
at the bottom. Access to the bulbs is obtained by removing the
screw and unclipping the rim and reflector assembly.
2   The headlamp bulb is held in position by a metal holder.
The bulb is removed by twisting the holder in the reflector. The
parking light (when fitted) is a push fit into the reflector.
3   The reflector can be removed from the rim by unclipping the
three wire clips that hold it in position against the rim.
4   The beam height can be adjusted by slackening the two
bolts which hold the headlamp shell in position. This allows the
beam to be adjusted up or down. Do not forget to tighten the
bolts after adjustment.
5   UK lighting regulations stipulate that the lighting system
must be arranged so that the light does not dazzle a person
standing in the same horizontal plane as the vehicle, at a
distance greater than 25 yards from the lamp, whose eye level is
not less than 3 feet 6 inches above that plane. It is easy to
approximate this setting by placing the machine 25 yards away
from a wall, on a level road, and setting the beam height so that
it is concentrated at the same height as the distance from the
centre of the headlamp to the ground. The rider must be seated
normally during this operation, and the pillion passenger, if
one is carried regularly.

**12 Speedometer indicator, high beam, turn indicator and neutral
light: bulb replacement**

1   Remove the two nuts and washers which secure the speedometer to the frame bracket.
2   The light holders are a push fit into the speedometer base.
The bulbs are of the bayonet type and are rated at 3W..

10.1 Note the rubber sealing washer

10.2 The bulb is of the bayonet type

11.1 Unclip the rim

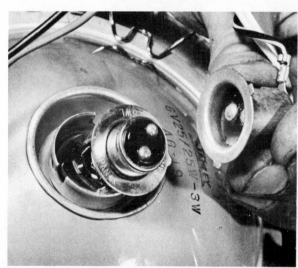

11.2a Release the metal holder to free the bulb

11.2b Pilot bulb is a push fit

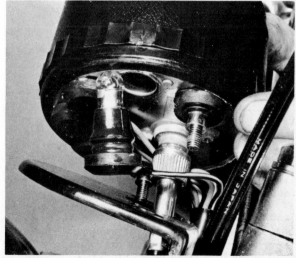

12.2 Bulb is push fit in base of speedometer

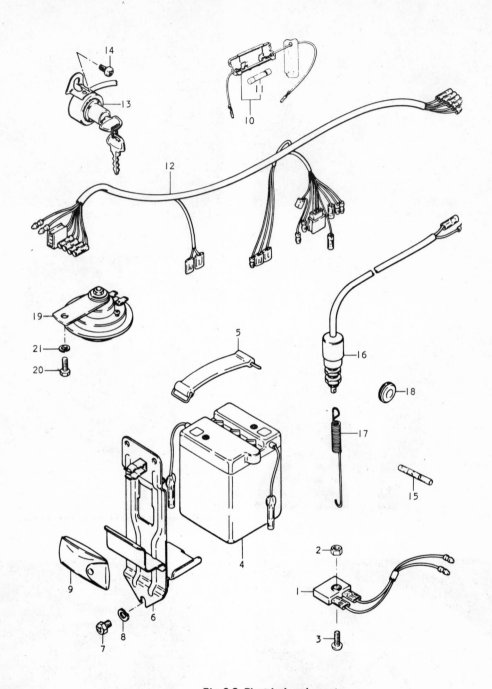

Fig. 6.3. Electrical equipment

1	Silicon rectifier	6	Battery holder	11	Fuse (15 amp)	16	Stop lamp switch
2	Nut	7	Battery holder screw - 3 off	12	Wiring harness	17	Return spring
3	Screw	8	Lockwasher - 3 off	13	Ignition switch assembly	18	Grommet
4	Battery	9	Tool kit	14	Screw - 2 off	19	Horn
5	Battery clamp	10	Fuse holder	15	Connector	20	Bolt
						21	Lockwasher

13.1a Undo the two screws to release the cover

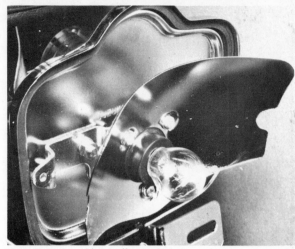

13.1b Note the rubber sealing washer

3   After bulb replacement, refit the speedometer to the frame bracket.

---

13 Rear and stop lamp: bulb and lens replacement

1   To remove the lens undo the two screws; note the rubber sealing washer behind the lens.
2   The twin filament bulb is of the staggered bayonet type and therefore can be replaced only one way.
3   When replacing the lens make sure to fit the rubber gasket. Do not overtighten the screws, or the plastic lens will crack.
4   If bulbs continue to blow, check that they are being earthed properly and also that the mudguard is not vibrating excessively (check securing bolts and washers etc).

---

14 Wiring: layout and examination

1   The wiring is colour-coded and will correspond with the accompanying wiring diagrams.
2   Visual inspection will show whether any breaks or frayed outer coverings are giving rise to short circuits. Another source of trouble may be the snap connectors, particularly where the connector has not been pushed home fully in the outer casing.
3   Intermittent short circuits can sometimes be traced to a chafed wire which passes through a frame member. Avoid tight bends in the wire or situations where the wire can become trapped or stretched between casings.

13.2 The twin filament stop/tail lamp bulb

15 Fault diagnosis: electrical system

Symptom	Cause	Remedy
Complete electrical failure	Blown fuse	Check wiring and electrical components for short circuit before fitting new 15 amp fuse. Check battery connections, also whether connections show signs of corrosion.
Dim lights, horn inoperative	Discharged battery	Re-charge battery with battery charger. Check whether generator is giving correct output.
Constantly blowing bulbs	Vibration, poor earth connection	Check security of bulb holders. Check earth return connections.

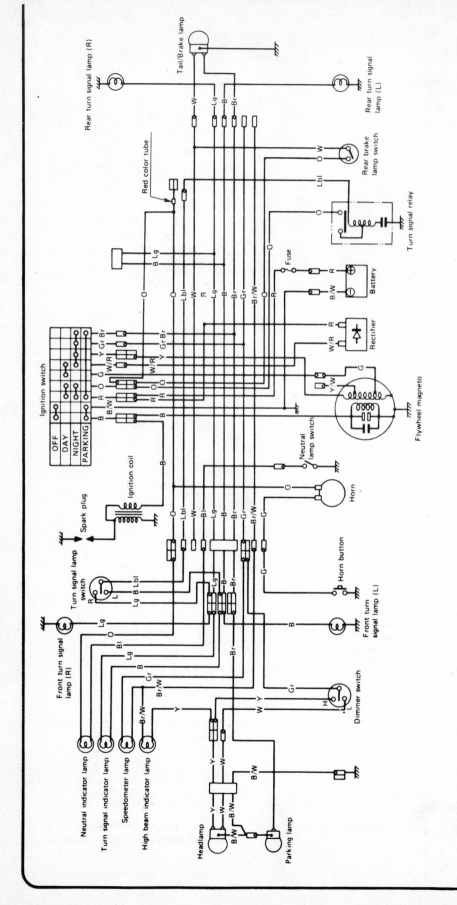

WIRE COLOR

B ..... Black	R ..... Red
Bl ..... Blue	W ..... White
Br ..... Brown	Y ..... Yellow
G ..... Green	B/W ..... Black with White tracer
Gr ..... Gray	Br/W ..... Brown with White tracer
Lbl ..... Light blue	W/R ..... White with Red tracer
Lg ..... Light green	Y/W ..... Yellow with White tracer
O ..... Orange	

Fig. 6.4. SUZUKI A50P wiring diagram

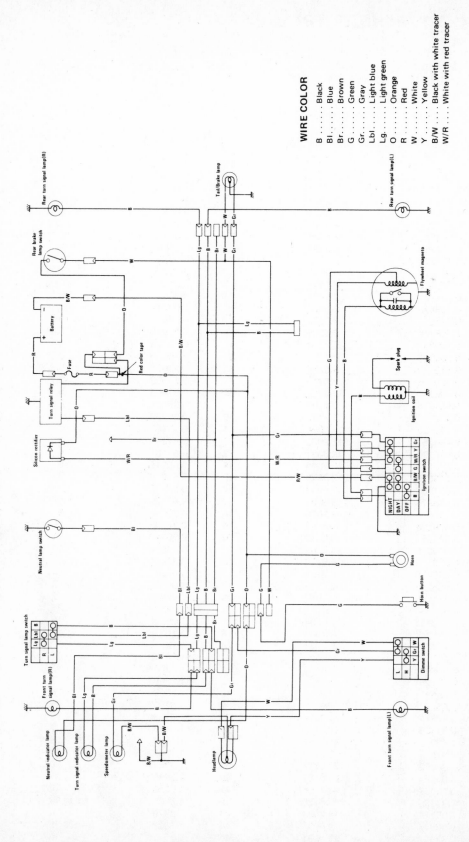

Fig. 6.5. SUZUKI A50 and AS50 Wiring diagrm

WIRE COLOR

B .... Black
Bl .... Blue
Br .... Brown
G .... Green
Gr .... Gray
Lbl .... Light blue
Lg .... Light green
O .... Orange
R .... Red
W .... White
Y .... Yellow
B/W .... Black with white tracer
W/R .... White with red tracer

Metric conversion tables

Inches	Decimals	Millimetres
1/64	0.015625	0.3969
1/32	0.03125	0.7937
3/64	0.046875	1.1906
1/16	0.0625	1.5875
5/64	0.078125	1.9844
3/32	0.09375	2.3812
7/64	0.109375	2.7781
1/8	0.125	3.1750
9/64	0.140625	3.5719
5/32	0.15625	3.9687
11/64	0.171875	4.3656
3/16	0.1875	4.7625
13/64	0.203125	5.1594
7/32	0.21875	5.5562
15/64	0.234275	5.9531
1/4	0.25	6.3500
17/64	0.265625	6.7469
9/32	0.28125	7.1437
19/64	0.296875	7.5406
5/16	0.3125	7.9375
21/64	0.328125	8.3344
11/32	0.34375	8.7312
23/64	0.359375	9.1281
3/8	0.375	9.5250
25/64	0.390625	9.9219
13/32	0.40625	10.3187
27/64	0.421875	10.7156
7/16	0.4375	11.1125
29/64	0.453125	11.5094
15/32	0.46875	11.9062
31/64	0.484375	12.3031
1/2	0.5	12.7000
33/64	0.515625	13.0969
17/32	0.53125	13.4937
35/64	0.546875	13.8906
9/16	0.5625	14.2875
37/64	0.578125	14.6844
19/32	0.59375	15.0812
39/64	0.609375	15.4781
5/8	0.625	15.8750
41/64	0.640625	16.2719
21/32	0.65625	16.6687
43/64	0.671875	17.0656
11/16	0.6875	17.4625
45/64	0.703125	17.8594
23/32	0.71875	18.2562
47/64	0.734375	18.6531
3/4	0.75	19.0500
49/64	0.765625	19.4469
25/32	0.78125	19.8437
51/64	0.796875	20.2406
13/16	0.8125	20.6375
53/64	0.828125	21.0344
27/32	0.84375	21.4312
55/64	0.859375	21.8281
7/8	0.875	22.2250
57/64	0.890625	22.6219
29/32	0.90625	23.0187
59/64	0.921875	23.4156
15/16	0.9375	23.8125
61/64	0.953125	24.2094
31/32	0.96875	24.6062
63/64	0.984375	25.0031

Millimetres to Inches	
mm	Inches
0.01	0.00039
0.02	0.00079
0.03	0.00118
0.04	0.00157
0.05	0.00197
0.06	0.00236
0.07	0.00276
0.08	0.00315
0.09	0.00354
0.1	0.00394
0.2	0.00787
0.3	0.1181
0.4	0.01575
0.5	0.01969
0.6	0.02362
0.7	0.02756
0.8	0.3150
0.9	0.03543
1	0.03937
2	0.07874
3	0.11811
4	0.15748
5	0.19685
6	0.23622
7	0.27559
8	0.31496
9	0.35433
10	0.39270
11	0.43307
12	0.47244
13	0.51181
14	0.55118
15	0.59055
16	0.62992
17	0.66929
18	0.70866
19	0.74803
20	0.78740
21	0.82677
22	0.86614
23	0.90551
24	0.94488
25	0.98425
26	1.02362
27	1.06299
28	1.10236
29	1.14173
30	1.18110
31	1.22047
32	1.25984
33	1.29921
34	1.33858
35	1.37795
36	1.41732
37	1.4567
38	1.4961
39	1.5354
40	1.5748
41	1.6142
42	1.6535
43	1.6929
44	1.7323
45	1.7717

Inches to Millimetres	
Inches	mm
0.001	0.0254
0.002	0.0508
0.003	0.0762
0.004	0.1016
0.005	0.1270
0.006	0.1524
0.007	0.1778
0.008	0.2032
0.009	0.2286
0.01	0.254
0.02	0.508
0.03	0.762
0.04	1.016
0.05	1.270
0.06	1.524
0.07	1.778
0.08	2.032
0.09	2.286
0.1	2.54
0.2	5.08
0.3	7.62
0.4	10.16
0.5	12.70
0.6	15.24
0.7	17.78
0.8	20.32
0.9	22.86
1	25.4
2	50.8
3	76.2
4	101.6
5	127.0
6	152.4
7	177.8
8	203.2
9	228.6
10	254.0
11	279.4
12	304.8
13	330.2
14	355.6
15	381.0
16	406.4
17	431.8
18	457.2
19	482.6
20	508.0
21	533.4
22	558.8
23	584.2
24	609.6
25	635.0
26	660.4
27	685.8
28	711.2
29	736.6
30	762.0
31	787.4
32	812.8
33	838.2
34	863.6
35	889.0
46	914.4

Index